Drive-Ins of Colorado

By Michael Kilgore

with Denver-area photos
by Kenneth James Mitchell

ID0896397

Published in the United States

ISBN 978-1-7333655-3-6

Library of Congress Control Number: 2020919594

First edition, October 2020

Table of Contents

Foreword

By Joe Bob Briggs

Colorado is a great drive-in state, and Michael Kilgore is a great drive-in historian.

The wide-open spaces of the West, the individualism of mom-and-pop operators who don't care what Hollywood is doing, the rugged beauty of the mountains, the plains, the valleys, the crooked roads to mines and gambling dens – all combine to make watching movies in the great outdoors of the Centennial State an infinitely varied experience that reflects the uniqueness of Colorado's peculiar mix of cultures and settings.

The Golden Age of the Colorado drive-in was the Fifties and the Sixties, but they survive into the present. And thanks to Michael's loving descriptions and detailed histories, they're certain to persist into the future.

The drive-in, like Pikes Peak and the Garden of the Gods, will never die.

Joe Bob Briggs has been America's foremost drive-in movie critic for over 30 years. In addition to a long-running syndicated newspaper column, he hosted *Joe Bob's Drive-In Theater* for almost a decade on The Movie Channel, then hosted *MonsterVision* on TNT for four years. Since 2018, he has presented *The Last Drive-In with Joe Bob Briggs* on Shudder. Joe Bob has written seven books, and his alter ego John Bloom has written two. To stay up to date with his latest appearances and writings, visit JoeBobBriggs.com.

Introduction

Welcome to the ultimate book of Colorado drive-in history, with the story of every ozoner that has ever existed in the state. It's a book that I've spent over 20 years creating.

Way back in the Internet 1.0 days, I founded Carload.com, a website dedicated to a dozen active Colorado drive-ins and what movies they were showing. Try to imagine how primitive life was back then. There was no Facebook, few drive-ins had their own web site, and every long-distance phone call cost money. Every week, a few calls and a little HTML editing were enough to promote all of these theaters.

As time passed, the need for a single Colorado drive-in site became a lot less obvious. So Carload expanded to cover active regional drive-ins, then every active ozoner in the US and Canada.

In 2017, I launched a Drive-In-A-Day Odyssey, visiting every remaining drive-in. (It was all done virtually; do I look like I'm made of money?) At most daily stops, I researched and wrote about that theater's story so far. Quite by accident, I caught the history bug.

Last year, I compiled and wrote *Drive-Ins of Route 66*, which contained the history of every drive-in that ever existed within a couple of miles of the Mother Road. Now I get to return to my adopted home state and write about every drive-in I've ever known here, plus dozens of others I never got to experience. I'm writing the book that I want to read, and I hope you enjoy reading it too.

Now let me answer some questions you might ask:

Why did you list drive-ins by city?

With a state full of dozens of drive-ins, there aren't many ways of arranging them to make them easy to find. Listing them alphabetically by name would mean adding extra stub entries for every alias for each one that changed their name. On the other hand, listing them alphabetically by city keeps regions together (the four drive-ins of Pueblo, for example) and reduces the number of stubs.

One more minor challenge is in the evolution of city limits. The Wadsworth Drive-In, for example, wasn't within the city limits of Arvada when it opened, but the site is there now. I've placed each drive-in's history in its current city or town, with stubs as needed for likely alternatives.

Why isn't my favorite in this book?

Either it was overlooked, or your favorite wasn't a drive-in theater in Colorado. Drive-in restaurants don't count (see the **Intermission: False Alarms**), and drive-in theaters across the border don't count (see the **Intermission: Over the Edge**). If you know something more, please send an email at mkilgore@Carload.com.

They did what to Native Americans?

Some of the city histories include some awful treatment of Native Americans. That's not good. Just because I have included some of those stories doesn't mean that I endorse them. Reciting old facts necessarily means restating old wrongs. Sorry about that.

My favorite drive-in is in this book, but why is its listing so short?

There are two main reasons:

1. Your favorite drive-in led an uneventful life. Alamosa's Ski-Hi Drive-In, which had the same owner when it opened as when it closed 47 years later, will be the first example you'll find here. Unless there's a fun anecdote to share, there isn't much to talk about.

2. I can't find enough information about it. For just a few of these, such as the Norwood Drive-In, all I know are the scant details in industry directories and any old aerial photos.

Dear reader, if you know more about a drive-in or have access to back issues of its town's newspaper, then you can let me know what I'm missing so I can update the next edition of this book. You can also let me know when you catch a mistake; there's probably at least one. Again, please drop me a line at mkilgore@Carload.com.

Thanks for reading,

Michael Kilgore
Carload.com

A Brief History of Drive-Ins

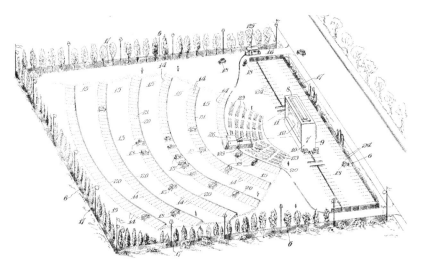

This illustration from Richard Hollinghead Jr.'s patent application shows the clamshell format that most drive-in theaters adopted.

The Shaky Start

Although silent-movie "drive-ins" had previously popped up now and then, Richard Hollingshead Jr. got the first patent for a drive in movie theater on June 1, 1933. What he really invented wasn't the outdoor theater, it was the drive-in ramp, which angled each car up to better point at the screen. You might also give him credit for the clamshell design for the viewing field, shown above.

Hollinghead's first location, opened June 6, 1933 near Camden NJ, was not a success. It was popular enough, but as with most 1930s drive-ins, its main problem was sound — no one had invented in-car speakers. Loudspeakers supplied the sound to drive-in patrons and often annoyed the neighbors. Another serious problem was that distributors weren't eager to rent films for it. Decades later, Hollingshead told the *Philadelphia Inquirer* that one of his first rentals "was three years old and cost us $400 for four days. The last time the film had run was in a little (theater) that paid $20 a week for it."

Hollingshead sold that Camden drive-in theater within three years to an indoor theater owner (with better film connections) who moved it to Union NJ. His patent didn't fare much better, as most competitors built similar sites without paying royalties. But potential drive-in builders weren't sure they could safely ignore the patent. That uncertainty, along with the early sound problems, left the drive-in as an unusual novelty. Fewer than two dozen permanent drive-in theaters were built in the first five years, although some small-town entrepreneurs operated short-lived versions using little more than bedsheets, loudspeakers, and film projectors. When the *Film Daily Year Book* published the first national drive-in theater list in 1942, it could find just 95 of them.

Walter McGhee, the manager of E. M. Loew's "Drive-In" in Providence RI, holds one of the "amplifiers" that attached to each car. Photo from *The Exhibitor*, Oct. 16, 1940.

The Postwar Explosion

World War II ended, and American soldiers returned home ready to start families and enjoy some entertainment. Their choices were live performance, radio, or the movies. Television stations lived in the big cities, and even where families could watch, it was an expensive novelty. A typical 1951 set could receive three black and white broadcasts on a screen smaller than most modern computer monitors and cost over $2500 in today's dollars. The only way to watch a movie was to see whatever was showing, a current film or a reissue, at a theater.

Back then, every factor lined up in favor of drive-ins. The rapidly growing population increasingly moved to suburbs and away from traditional downtown theaters, where parking could be difficult or expensive. Adults used to dress up for a night at an indoor theater, and families with children needed to find babysitters. Outdoor movies could start at a decent hour because daylight time wasn't much of a thing yet. Car ownership rapidly became ubiquitous. Hollywood slowly switched to movies in color, even as it continued to create films suitable for the whole family. Plentiful cheap land at the edge of town beckoned developers.

An important factor in the growth of drive-ins was the invention of in-car speakers that could be hung from a window. Photo from an ad in *Motion Picture Herald*.

The number of drive-ins grew steadily, but the real explosion came after October 1949 when the US

Supreme Court ruled, in effect, that Hollinghead's ramp could not be patented. In one year, the number of US drive-ins more than doubled, from about 750 in 1949 to over 1700 in 1950. That number would have grown quickly higher, but in September 1950, as the Korean War flared, the US National Production Authority began requiring its approval to use certain building materials for entertainment facilities. Despite that speed bump, drive-in construction resumed normally within a couple of years, and the drive-in population grew to over 4300 by 1955. After that high point, that number leveled out for the next decade.

The Long Decline

After the drive-in population plateaued, most of the factors that led to their growth peeled away one by one. Television expanded to almost every city, and TV set prices dropped from unthinkable to simply expensive. Families snapped them up; 83 percent of American homes had TV in 1958, up from a mere 9 percent in 1950.

At all theaters, fewer films worked for the whole family; most explored more mature topics, and some were too childish for grown-ups to enjoy. Casual wear became acceptable at indoor theaters, and there were more of them close to home near suburban shopping centers. National adoption of Daylight Saving Time in 1967 sliced a crucial hour off already limited drive-in schedules.

Movie-viewing at home became more convenient. Home Box Office launched in 1972, the first of a wave of commercial-free, uncut movie channels for home viewing. Perhaps the final, most lethal drive-in killer was the video cassette recorder. As VCRs dropped in price, video rental stores popped up. A family could line up a double- or triple-feature with homemade snacks for less than the cost of a night out.

The ultimate nemesis of drive-ins was television. First any kind of TV, then color TV, then cable TV, then TV movie channels, then VCRs for playing movies on TVs. Each advance carved off another fraction of the drive-ins' audience.

Photo by tomislav medak.

Many drive-ins reacted by trying to provide viewers with an experience they couldn't get on television. In the mid-1950s, that meant wide-screen movies, and most pre-existing drive-ins added wings to their screens. Westerns and other family fare faded. As the typical car became less likely to include children, drive-in movie-makers shifted their attention to teenagers and young adults. In the 1960s and 1970s, that often meant horror or titillation films, which were eventually labeled as R-rated. Some drive-ins went even further, showing softcore sexy R movies or even hardcore adult films.

As cities and suburbs expanded, they often encircled previously remote drive-ins. Whenever a developer wanted a contiguous piece of land for a shopping mall or a housing tract, he could offer to buy a drive-in. Some landowners had figured this out decades earlier, offering short-term leases to drive-in theatres while planning to cash out once their parcels became valuable. Combine that with the dwindling crowds and neighborhood pressure against X-rated movies, selling out was often the landowner's best choice.

21st Century Rediscovery

Most drive-ins that persisted past the year 2000 were either popular in small but not tiny towns (about 5,000-10,000 people), or were in metropolitan areas stuck on pieces of land that were unappealing for other uses. For the survivors, a few new factors started tilting back in their direction.

Disney always produced family-friendly movies, and it started a trend with Best Picture nominee *Beauty and the Beast* (1991). Hoping for similar success, other filmmakers returned to making animated movies that the whole family could enjoy. Studios expanded production of comic book adaptations and other cartoonish action movies, so drive-ins once again had a product to sell to both children and their parents. The FM radio transmitter supplemented and frequently replaced in-car speakers since most cars now had FM stereo radios. Patrons enjoyed richer movie audio than they had from a single, tinny in-car speaker, and drive-in owners didn't have to maintain and replace speakers every month.

Of all the changes that led to the drive-in theater renaissance, none were more important than FM stereo sound. Once it was reasonable to assume that every car had an FM radio, drive-in operators could switch to a cheap audio delivery system and patrons could enjoy a superior sound experience. © Depositphotos / Ensuper

Near the close of the last century, when the US Postal Service asked its users to vote on the topic that best commemorated the 1950s, they were surprised that the big winner was drive-in movies. Postwar baby boomer children had become parents themselves and grew nostalgic for the advantages and fun of the drive-in. Surviving drive-ins showed an uptick in attendance around the turn of the century.

But that didn't mean they were out of the woods. Almost no new drive-ins were being built, and every year, a few drive-ins closed as their aging owner-managers cashed out, retired, or both.

Drive-In Economics

Let me pause for a moment to describe a typical drive-in theater's sources of income. In the early days, drive-ins often rented or even purchased and kept the ticket proceeds. In 1954, concession stand sales accounted

Bagged food behind sliding glass panels in a cafeteria-style line — these concession-stand staples have been around for over 60 years. And they're still there at the 88 Drive-In in Commerce City. 2013 photo by the author.

Another long-lasting drive-in staple is the reminder to visit the concession stand, played before the show starts and at intermission. 2013 photo of the 88 Drive-In by the author.

for just 22% of the average drive-in's income. Those days are long gone. Today, a very high percentage of each ticket goes to the movie's distributor, so modern drive-ins make most of their money through the concession stand.

In effect, most drive-in theaters operate as seasonal outdoor restaurants with an entertainment theme. They're popular and a lot more fun, but keeping that in mind, you can see how it's hard to get rich by running a drive-in. It also explains why some drive-in owners get really cheesed when patrons bring in their own food. The best drive-ins sell food so good that you'd look forward to choosing it for dinner. Even for the bad ones, I still make a point to buy popcorn and soda, a drive-in's most profitable products. But I have digressed long enough. Back to history.

The Digital Imperative

Theatrical digital movie projection, using hard drives instead of reels of film, was first demonstrated in 1999. After 15 years of tweaking the format and planning a new distribution system, Hollywood decided to switch.

The word came down from studios that they would no longer spend $5 million or more per movie to print a limited number of copies on fragile, heavy film. They required all theaters to convert to digital projection so they could use easier-to-ship, reusable hard drives instead.

Drive-ins always needed powerful film projectors to show films. Their larger screens sat farther away than indoor theaters', and ambient city light interfered more than a darkened room. To comply with Hollywood's demand, they needed special, expensive digital projectors. As I just mentioned, drive-ins typically don't clear a ton of money, so many of them feared that they'd have to close when the last film versions of movies disappeared.

In 2013, Honda spotlighted these owners' plight through Project Drive-In, where fans could vote for their favorite theater. Honda awarded projectors to nine winners, and the contest drew public attention to the drive-ins that didn't win.

When the final wave of digital conversion hit soon after, some drive-ins shut down, but not as many as some had feared. And here's the thing — those that survived found that whatever didn't kill them made them stronger.

The digital system has its benefits. Picture quality is always excellent. "Prints" of any movie are easily available. Drive-in screens can show broadcast sports or huge video games. And having invested all that money in equipment, today's drive-ins have a stronger incentive to stay open year after year. Brand-new drive-ins are being built, and new-wave "pop-up" boutique drive-ins thrive in converted parking lots.

The steady pressure of rising land value continues to close a few drive-ins every year. But some of the original attractions of a drive-in are now causing about as many to pop up in their place. Substitute FM radio sound for a loudspeaker and once again, all a theatrical entrepreneur really needs is a projector, a screen, and a parking lot.

The Blue Starlite Mini Urban (sic) Drive-In Theater in Minturn is a great example of the new style of popup drive-in. Almost anyone could replicate its small digital projector and inflatable screen. It would be much harder for just any-one to replicate its cool attitude. 2017 photo by the author.

A Brief History of Colorado's Drive-Ins

For the first dozen years of their existence, drive-in theaters got a cold shoulder from Colorado. Some of that was literal; Leonard Albertini later told the *Denver Post*, "Everyone said a drive-in would never go here because of the cold weather." More about him shortly.

Another huge factor in the drive-ins' delayed debut in the state was the uncertainty over Hollinghead's patent, discussed in the previous chapter. His company licensed that patent, and its clients received an exclusive territory along with the right to do business. Many of the state's first dozen drive-ins, though not all of them, were officially sanctioned in this way.

One positive side-effect was that Colorado's drive-in neighbors were spared a common annoyance at many 1930s drive-ins — loudspeakers pumping out movie sound. After World War II, owners equipped their drive-ins with in-car speakers as a matter of course.

Beachheads in the Big Cities

The first Colorado drive-ins were all near its largest cities. The very first was built by Leonard Albertini, who came to Denver with an official "Park-In" franchise and spent months trying to get a local backer. In late 1946, Harris Wolfberg, founder and president of a large local

theater chain, took the bait.
Wolfberg formed a
corporation with Albertini
and a group that included
Quigg Newton, who was
elected mayor of Denver in
May 1947. They invested
over $150,000 to build the
structure known at first as
"Drive-In" on East Colfax
Avenue in Aurora.
Colorado's drive-in history
began on July 4, 1947.

What became the East
Drive-In in Aurora was
called simply "Drive-In" in
its grand opening ad in the
July 4, 1947 issue of the
Denver Post.

As the future East
Drive-In neared
completion, Loyd Files and
associates began building
the Starlite near his auto wrecking yard in Grand
Junction. It opened less than a month after Aurora's
drive-in.

The Starlite and Aurora's drive-in were both instant
successes, playing to packed houses; the Aurora drive-in
paid for itself in little over a year. Other entrepreneurs
took notice.

In Pueblo, Lionel Semon had announced plans for
his drive-in within a week of Aurora's opener, though
construction didn't begin until the winter of 1947.

Similarly, in Colorado Springs, Cy Lee and Paul
Rothman bought a Park-In franchise and started building
a couple miles east of town in March 1948. The Starlight
(often written as Starlite) opened there on June 30.

Meanwhile in Denver, Wolfberg immediately began
looking around to see how many of these money
machines he could build. Eventually promoting the
Compass drive-in chain, he built the West in Lakewood

and acquired what would become the North in Westminster (long story) in 1948, and added the South in Englewood a year later. Aurora's drive-in became the East.

(Almost) Every Town Joins In

As I wrote in the previous chapter, the largest surge in drive-in construction came between October 1949, when Hollinghead's ramp lost its patent, and September 1950, when the Korean War led to building material restrictions. Colorado was no exception; 16 of its drive-ins opened in that span of less than a year. Many of those were in smaller towns such as Sterling, Montrose, and Lamar.

By the middle of the 1950s, more budding theater men and women were building drive-ins even in the smallest of towns. Norwood (population ~350) and Dove Creek (~750) both built drive-ins in 1953. Ignacio (population ~580) and Hotchkiss (~700) got theirs in 1955.

Larger metropolitan areas also continued adding more drive-ins, and by 1958, 80% of all the drive-ins that would ever exist in Colorado had been built. And a few of them had already closed.

What Do You Like In Motion Pictures;

Musicals, Westerns, Dramas, Mysteries, News and Sports, Lots of Cartoons or Complete Shows of Cartoons?

We would like to show the types of movie entertainment you prefer.

We therefore request that you tell us in person or by mail the type of picture you like and want to see.

ADDRESS

Buckskin

Drive-In Theatre

Box 366   Ignacio, Colo   Phone 2089

I PREFER THE FOLLOWING MOVIES:

Signed: ....

Address: ....

(Clip this coupon and paste to postal card)

Before it opened, the owners of Ignacio's drive-in took out a newspaper ad to ask the locals what kind of movies they wanted.

The Long Decline, Colorado Style

Nationally, the two major culprits in killing off drive-ins were increased competition from television (then HBO, then VCRs) and rising land prices. Colorado added a third: the boom-and-bust cycle of mining. Whether it was coal in Walsenburg, uranium in Naturita, or oil shale in Delta, when the minerals ran out, so did a lot of spending money.

The theater chains along the Front Range added a few drive-ins in the 1960s, largely chasing new suburbanites. There were also a few outliers in smaller towns, including Buena Vista (1967) and Lamar (1973). The ultimate outlier was in Burlington, built in 1976, three years after any other drive-in in the state.

Meanwhile, other drive-ins were closing. Although the majority of Colorado's drive-ins survived into the 1980s, fewer than two dozen made it to 1990. In big cities, they were swallowed by urban development. Near small towns, they were often left as vacant fields; there are some overgrown 65-year-old ramps out there if you know where to look for them.

New Drive-Ins for the New Normal

After a gap of almost 40 years, in 2015, the first 21st Century drive-in in Colorado popped up in northern Denver, where a trade show marketplace saw what it could do with a section of its underused parking lot. The next year, the guy who was running a successful pop-up drive-in in Austin TX wisely began taking his summers in a riverside park in Minturn.

Both of these newest drive-ins use FM stereo sound exclusively. (That's not so unusual; most of the state's

The Denver Mart Drive-In, opened in 2015, doesn't allow walk-ins, but it offers a dozen lawn chairs for patrons who want to get out of their cars. 2017 photo by the author.

other active drive-ins also use radio sound.) Neither of them use any ramps; the last ramps built in Colorado were in Burlington.

In the year of this writing, the COVID-19 virus has changed a great many things. Hanging out at the snack bar became a really bad idea. Even cars are required to social distance from each other. And pop-up drive-ins are, well, popping up all over. It would be foolish to predict which of this year's new drive-ins, if any, will still be in operation in post-vaccine era, just as it would be premature to estimate when that era will begin.

What I hope is that Colorado's active drive-ins will continue well into the new century. As more patrons learn how nice it is to feel the state's cool evening breezes while enjoying movies from the comfort and familiarity of their cars, I hope this also encourages the construction of more new facilities. For a relaxing, fun outing, nothing beats the drive-in.

Colorado's 85 Drive-Ins, Ordered by Opening Date

(Listed as opening date, drive-in name, drive-in city. Active drive-ins in **bold**)

July 4, 1947 - East / East 70, Aurora
Aug. 2, 1947 - Starlite, Grand Junction
May 20, 1948 - Pueblo, Pueblo
June 30, 1948 - Starlight / Starlite, Colorado Springs
July 17, 1948 - West, Lakewood
July 17, 1948 - Motorena / North, Westminster
Aug. 14, 1948 - Greeley, Greeley
Aug. 21, 1948 - Motorena, Greeley
Sept. 22, 1948 - La Junta, La Junta
Oct. 1, 1948 - Motorena, Boulder
Oct. 5, 1948 - Sunset, Fort Collins
May 10, 1949 - Skylite / Big Sky, Delta
June 23, 1949 - Lake, Pueblo
July 1, 1949 - South, Englewood
July 31, 1949 - Independent, Cortez
Aug. 4, 1949 - Sunset, Canon City
October? 1949 - Peak, Trinidad
April 15, 1950 - Starlite, Sterling
April 8, 1950 - Kar-Vu, Brighton
April 19, 1950 - **Star**, Montrose
May 5, 1950 - 8th Street, Colorado Springs
May 12, 1950 - Groy / Knox, Salida
May 18, 1950 - Bauer's / Valley, Fort Morgan
May 25, 1950 - Kar-Vu, Lamar
May 26, 1950 - Northside, Colorado Springs
June 1, 1950 - Ski-Hi, Alamosa
June? 1950 - Star-Vu, Longmont
June 23, 1950 - Basin / Knox / Bell, Durango

July 7, 1950 - Chief, Rifle
July 13, 1950 - Monaco, Denver
Sept. 3, 1950 - Arroyo / Arroya, Cortez
Sept. 12, 1950 - Canyon, Grand Junction
June 1, 1951 - Luv-Vu / Motorena, Loveland
July 1, 1951 - Brush, Brush
July 6, 1951 - Lake Shore, Edgewater
Aug. 17, 1951 - **Mesa**, Pueblo
March 21, 1952 - Chief, Grand Junction
April 25, 1952 - Corral, Hudson
1952? - T.A. Buss / Norwood, Norwood
March 26, 1953 - Starlite, Rocky Ford
May 15, 1953 - L&L Motor Vu / Star-Lite, Louisville
May 15, 1953 - Lake Estes, Estes Park
May 22, 1953 - Auto Vu, Dove Creek
June 6, 1953 - Valley, Denver
June 12, 1953 - Hicks on 96 / 96 / East, Pueblo
July? 1953 - Roundup, La Jara
July 9, 1953 - Holiday, Boulder
March 13, 1954 - Uranium, Naturita
April 17, 1954 - Centennial, Littleton
May 8, 1954 - Wadsworth Indoor / A-Best /
        Mountain-Vu, Arvada
Aug. 6, 1954 - Sunset / Romantic / Motor Vu, Craig
Aug. 11, 1954 - Evans, Denver
March 11, 1955 - **Tru Vu**, Delta
April 8, 1955, Aircadia, Colorado Springs
April 10, 1955 - Buckskin, Ignacio
April 16, 1955 - Rocket, Grand Junction
April 21, 1955 - Tsaya, Cortez
May 4, 1955 - Julesburg / Arrow, Julesburg
May 14, 1955 - Frontier, Center
July 1, 1955 - **Star**, Monte Vista
July 22, 1955 - Island Acres, Gunnison
July 28, 1955, Sky Vue, Colorado Springs

Aug. 19, 1955 - Valley, Hotchkiss

June 29, 1956 - Vista Vue / Vista View, Fountain

Aug. 12, 1956 - 47 / Outdoor Cinema /
       Castle Rock, Castle Rock

March 10, 1957 - Rocket, Durango

June 7, 1957 - Paonia, Paonia

June 15, 1957 - Monument, Grand Junction

July 5, 1957 - Sunset / Apache / Kar-Vu, Springfield

June 30, 1961 - North Star, Thornton

July 5, 1963 - Trail, Walsenburg

May 25, 1966 - Havana, Aurora

March 23, 1967 - Nor-West, Broomfield

June 8, 1967 - Pines, Loveland

June 14, 1967 - West Colfax, Lakewood

July 13, 1967 - **Comanche**, Buena Vista

April 10, 1968 - **Starlight / Holiday Twin**,
       Fort Collins

Aug. 2, 1969 - Falcon, Colorado Springs

Aug. 12, 1971, **East 88th Avenue / 88**, Commerce City

April 12, 1972 - Arapahoe, Greenwood Village

June 22, 1973 - Arrow, Lamar

July 18, 1973 - Cinderella Twin, Sheridan

May? 1976 - Burlington, Burlington

June 12, 2015 - **Denver Mart**, Denver

July 6, 2016 - **Blue Starlite**, Minturn

Drive-Ins by City

Alamosa

As a tourist, I always think of Alamosa as the gateway to the Great Sand Dunes National Park. But since the railroads appeared, it's been the rail hub of the San Luis Valley. The Rio Grande Scenic Railroad still runs excursion trains in the summer months.

Ski-Hi Drive-In

Opened: June 1, 1950

Closed: Sept. 5, 1996

Capacity: 400 cars

In late 1949, Hubbard & Murphy Theatres, which already owned the indoor Grove and Rialto theaters in Alamosa, employed George Frantz to design and build the Sky-Hi a couple of miles west of town on the highway to Monte Vista. The process took over six months, and the cost estimates grew from $60,000 to $100,000. The *Alamosa Daily Courier* described the difficulty in finding enough gravel to cover the field and in finding the

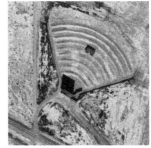

The Ski-Hi in 1960. © HistoricAerials.com, used by permission

THANK YOU, SAN LUIS VALLEY
FOLKS, FOR YOUR WONDERFUL
Patronage Last Night. Although All the Facilities Were Not
Quite Completed for Our Opening, We Assure You That
Within A Few Days Everything Will Be Operating in Tip
Top Shape to Give You Finer Service!

The Ski-Hi ran a grand opening followup ad
in the next day's *Alamosa Daily Courier* as a
combination thanks and apology

55-foot poles to support "Moon-Glo" lights. Frantz told
the *Daily Courier*, "There wouldn't be any fun in my line
of work of we didn't encounter a few problems. The fun
comes in having the satisfaction of seeing these problems
solved."

"Follow the Flares to the Ski-Hi" was the slogan for
the grand opening on Thursday, June 1, 1950. Red flares
lined the road from Alamosa to the drive-in, and a large
fireworks display marking the opening. More than 1000
cars came to watch, so most of them were turned away
by highway patrolmen called in to handle traffic. Many
parked on the shoulders of the highway to watch the fireworks at least.

Perhaps inspired by the reaction to opening night,
the Ski-Hi continued to shoot off fireworks three times a
year. Everything else also stayed pretty much the same.
The windshield cleaners moved from the box office to
their own building at the back of the ramps in 1954. The
Ski-Hi's owners' company changed names a couple of
times, but the drive-in was never sold. In 1996, Murphy
Theatres announced plans to build an indoor six-screen
theatre on the site of the drive-in, and after two "Nostalgia weeks" showing *A Very Brady Sequel*, the Ski-Hi
Drive-In closed on the Thursday after Labor Day 1996.

Arvada

Fast-growing Arvada is the 7th most populous city in Colorado as of this writing. Its population was expanding rapidly during the 1950s when its drive-in arrived, from less than 2400 in 1950 to over 19,000 at the end of the decade. My favorite district there is the historic Olde Town Arvada, located just a bit north of where the drive-in used to live.

Wadsworth Indoor / A-Best / Mountain Vu Drive-In

Opened: May 8, 1954

Closed: Dec. 1, 1981

Capacity: 1000 cars and 502 seats

Lem K. Lee, president of Lee Theatres, was riding high in 1953 when he announced plans to build the Wadsworth. He had built Greeley's Motorena Drive-In, Denver's Monaco Drive-In, and two in Colorado Springs, but now he was returning to the town where he had run his first indoor theater after moving from Oklahoma to Colorado.

Motion Picture Herald and *Boxoffice* both ran splashy features on the Wadsworth's debut, calling

The grand opening marquee, as printed in the *1954-55 Theatre Catalog*.

The Wadsworth's grand opening ad in the *Denver Post* showed how indoor patrons could see the wide screen across the viewing field.

its 103x69-foot screen "the largest yet made without a seam." The drive-in's main innovation was an enclosed, glass-fronted auditorium with 502 seats, accounting for the "Indoor" part of the name. Lee's plan was to make this a year-round theater.

The drive-in was supposed to open on May 1, but a huge snowstorm hit the Denver area, forcing a delay. That may have been a bad omen. In November that year, Lee set up a kids' Saturday matinee, bringing down a projector to the auditorium and using a screen to cover its front. Was that smart thinking or desperation?

In August 1955, a squabble among investors forced the sale of the Wadsworth at public auction. The next spring, Merf Evans formed A-Best Drive-In, Inc., which signed a 10-year lease and renamed the drive-in. At the time, they planned to convert the indoor auditorium to concession stands, but by October, the A-Best was back to holding Saturday matinees there.

Change swept through yet again in March 1957, when the *Denver Post* announced the opening of the Mountain Vu, which was "the former A-Best Drive-In … completely redecorated by the new management." But

The 1954-55 *Theatre Catalog* showed what it looked like to watch a drive-in movie from an indoor auditorium.

financial troubles remained. Wadsworth Electric and Gas sued A-Best for payment that summer. In June 1958, A-Best filed for bankruptcy, closed the drive-in, and advertised it for sale.

Vera Cockrill, who owned the Denham Theater in downtown Denver, bought the drive-in, remodeled "the entire plant" including a new car speaker system, and reopened it as the Wadsworth on May 1, 1959. That was exactly five years after it was ready to open in the first place, making me wonder what had become broken or obsolete so quickly. Its reopening ad promised the brightest screen (coated with Manco-Vision) in the Denver area, a new children's playground, and a new concession stand.

Anyway, the new Wadsworth calmed down after that. Wolfberg Theatres took over in 1967, and Commonwealth Theatres bought out Wolfberg in 1979. The Wadsworth offered its final program on Dec. 1, 1981.

Aurora

Aurora, the third-most populous city in Colorado, is still a Denver suburb, as it was when it birthed the state's first drive-in. Unlike many other cities, Aurora didn't allow flea markets at its drive-ins, voting them down in June 1977. The city council claimed that flea markets cause traffic problems and compete with garage sales.

East / East 70 Drive-In

Opened: July 4, 1947

Closed: 1994

Capacity: 780 cars

I'm so glad that an accident of alphabetization placed the East so close to the front of this book. In many ways, it lit the drive-in fire that spread across the state.

The Denver Drive-In Theatre Corp. was led by local movie patriarch Harris P. Wolfberg and soon-to-be Denver mayor Quigg Newton. With other investors, they built Colorado's first drive-in theater on East Colfax across from the Fitzsimons Army Hospital. Its completion date slipped from June 1 to June 15 to June 25 before finally opening on Independence Day. That night, a traffic jam extended over a mile west of the drive-in along Colfax through Aurora's business district. Management soon added a second box office to

The first outdoor screen in Colorado, just before the drive-in opened. Photo by Greg Albertini.

handle the capacity crowds.

When it opened, the drive-in was un-named, as was common for Richard Hollings-head Jr.'s "Park-In The-atre" franchises. Ushers used flashlights to guide cars to their places on the ramps. A contractor, Lem Lee, ran the conces-sion stand. Manager Leonard Albertini lived with his wife in an apartment at the base of the screen tower.

During winter months, Wolf-berg's Compass drive-ins would sometimes rent their marquees for advertising, as shown in the February 1958 issue of Frontier Airlines' *Sunliner News*.

Aurora's drive-in was a huge success, and Wolfberg began looking for other Denver-area sites to expand; he decided on directional names for what became the Compass chain. Within a week after reopening for the 1948 season, Albertini's drive-in began advertising as the East.

The next few decades were fairly quiet. The East added a Ferris wheel in 1951. In August 1954, a storm uprooted several concrete foundations for speaker poles. In September 1955, President Dwight Eisenhower was treated at Fitzsimons after a heart attack. *Denver Post* photographer Dave Mathias found a high spot at the East (it's unclear whether it was up the screen tower or just atop the projection building) and took the first photo of Eisenhower outdoors after treatment. Another storm in 1960 blew away part of a fence.

The drive-in was modernized before the 1965 season, complete with a wide screen, an upgraded sound system, and a rebuilt snack bar / projection booth containing

After adding the enhanced clarity of 70mm film, Wolfberg began calling this drive-in the East 70, usually with a "New" in front to emphasize the change. Photo courtesy of Aurora History Museum, Aurora, Colorado.

70mm projectors. Wolfberg renamed it the East 70 to underscore the use of this larger, clearer film.

A year later, the East hosted an AM radio sound experiment using the "Minicast" system. It didn't last very long, but while it did, neighbors in nearby apartments could listen as well as watch out their windows.

Before the 1990 season, Steven Vannoy and partner Philip Simms took over the East and tried to clean it up. They quickly came into conflict with next-door neighbor Paul Tauer, who happened to be mayor of Aurora. Vannoy had big ideas for sock hops, collectible shows and other events, but the city turned down every special-use permit request. Vannoy sold out the following year, and soon published a best-selling parenting book, *The 10 Greatest Gifts I Give My Children*.

Joel Boldrey, president of Summit Theatre Corp., took over in 1991, and I can't find any further

The East 70 was no longer "New" but it was still across from Fitzsimons in this 1992 photo by Kenneth James Mitchell.

transactions for the East. In August 1994, two teenagers working the front ticket booth were nearly killed by a knife-wielding robber. The assailant was later apprehended, tried, and convicted, but the drive-in closed for good just a few weeks after the attack.

The East's screen tower always displayed its original name, "Drive-In Theatre". 1984 photo by Kenneth James Mitchell.

The Havana's gala opening ad in the *Denver Post* featured that spire, part of "Colorado's first outdoor motion picture theatre in a garden atmosphere." 1979 photo by Maritza Bachmann.

Havana Drive-In

Opened: May 25, 1966

Closed: Sept. 27, 1981

Capacity: 1400 cars

The Havana got its start in early 1965. Vera Cockrill, the owner of the Wadsworth Drive-In and the indoor Denham Theatre, and Charles Reagan, a longtime friend of her late husband, bought a then-recently built indoor theater from Colorado Amusement Corp. Part of the deal was some land for a drive-in. Cockrill immediately announced that she would build that drive-in, on Havana Street between Mississippi and Florida avenues.

Construction began in mid-March that year, but then state legislators threw a monkey wrench – a law opting in to daylight saving time. Cockrill halted construction in April to see just how bad DST would be for drive-ins in the area. Those effects must have been manageable, because work restarted the following spring.

An old-fashioned writer might have said that the Havana was designed with a woman's touch. A Chinese Elm hedge surrounded the grounds, which included landscaped park-like setting, flower beds, two playgrounds for children of different age groups, and a fountain and reflection pool. The projection booth held both 70mm and standard 35mm projectors.

After one successful season, Cockrill leased all of her theaters except the Denham to Wolfberg Theatres, who added the drive-ins to its Compass chain. The rest of the Havana's life was fairly uneventful. Commonwealth took over the Compass chain in 1979, and it closed the Havana after the 1981 season.

Boulder

Boulder was named for Boulder Creek, which was named for the large boulders next to it. In 1861, the state legislature made it the home of the University of Colorado, though it didn't open until 16 years later.

Fewer than 20,000 people lived there when its first drive-ins arrived, but there were more than 80,000 when the last one went dark.

Holiday Drive-In

Opened: July 9, 1953

Moved: July 9, 1969

Closed: Sept. 10, 1989

Capacity: 600 cars, then 850 cars

Wilbur Williams and Claude Graves built the first Holiday on 18 acres near 28th and Pennsylvania streets. Well, at least they paid for it; Tom Griffing's drive-in builders did the actual construction. As it was going up, C. L. Onsgard won the naming contest, scoring a lifetime pass to the Holiday.

The new drive-in had a 70 by 45-foot screen affixed to a larger screen tower. The Holiday sign, looking about the same as it always would, divided the double entrance and exit lanes. Stone flower boxes and ornamental light poles lined the path from 28th Street to the box office, which was made of ornamental stone from Lyons. A large cement patio stretched out of the projection-concession stand. Soon after opening, they added a playground just in front of the screen.

In March 1962, an insurance inspector checking the screen tower found that a teenage boy had hanged himself there. One month

After the Holiday closed, its sign deteriorated for a while, as shown in this photo by Tadson Bussey.

Thanks to a grant from the Colorado Historical Society, the restored Holiday sign still attracts attention on US 36 in northwest Boulder. 2020 photo by the author.

later, a 60-mph wind knocked down and demolished the tower. The drive-in stayed closed for two years until reopening with a steel screen just before the 1964 season.

In 1966, Highland Theatres incorporated in Boulder, starting with five theaters including both local drive-ins, buying the Holiday from Williams and Graves. Three years later, as development made the Holiday's original location desirable for other development, Highland moved the drive-in to the northwest side of town.

The Holiday brought its old sign with it when it reopened in July 1969. A year later, Highland added a second screen with a smaller viewing field. The drive-in rolled along well into the 1990s, ending its run with a live trapeze act.

The afterlife of the site was as eventful as the drive-in had been. Although scheduled for demolition almost immediately after closing, the concession building was still sheltering transients in 1996. The old Holiday sign slowly deteriorated. Finally, Boulder Housing Partners developed the old site into affordable housing. The nonprofit restored the sign and shifted it closer to US 36. And it created a green space, Holiday Park, just where the old viewing field had been.

Motorena Drive-In

Opened: Oct. 1, 1948

Closed: Sept. 6, 1977

Capacity: 666 cars

The folks who opened the Motorena in Westminster a few months earlier rushed to complete Boulder's version before the close of the 1948 season. It opened three miles east of the city limits on "the Arapahoe Highway," (Colorado 7), across from the Valmont power plant.

The Motorena's ramps were paved with oil, and could hold exactly 666 cars pointed at the 52x48-foot screen. "Moon glow" lighting provided enough background for patrons to get around. Irving Gilman, general manager of the Boulder Drive-In Theater Corporation, told the Boulder *Daily Camera* that it was okay for drivers to shift their position for the best viewing angle. "Some patrons, new to drive-ins,

The Motorena in 1963, when it still had only one screen. © Historicaerials.com, used by permission.

Spotted letters and the comedy / tragedy masks were trademarks of all Motorena drive-ins, as shown in this ad in the *Boulder Daily Camera*.

seem to think that after an usher shows them to their place, they are not allowed to move their cars at all." Richard Koenig managed the Motorena during its first few years.

Before the 1959 season, Wilbur Williams, co-owner of the Holiday, told *Boxoffice* that he planned to open both the Holiday and Motorena in late March. I'm not sure whether he bought into the corporation that had owned the Motorena or simply purchased the drive-in in the mid-1950s. I imagine that Williams was glad to have both drive-ins when the Holiday's screen was knocked out of commission for two years. In mid-summer 1962, the Motorena was also briefly closed for screen repairs.

The new Highland Theatres corporation, based in Boulder, launched in 1966, buying all of the theaters owned by Williams and Claude Graves. Highland added a second screen to the Motorena in late 1970, advertising it as the Motorena Twin. Highland merged with Cooper, and the combined entity saw the close of the Motorena at the end of the 1977 season.

Brighton

Denver real estate agent Daniel Carmichael started buying land around what was then known as Hughes Station in the early 1880s. When he incorporated the town in 1887, he named it after his wife's birthplace, Brighton Beach NY. Today it's the seat of Adams County, even though a bit of it crosses over into Weld County.

Kar-Vu Drive-In

Opened: April 8, 1950

Closed: 1980

Capacity: 350 cars

In April 1949, Elden Menagh, owner of the indoor Star in Fort Lupton, announced that was going to build a 550-car drive-in in Greeley. A month later, he changed his mind, buying a Fort Lupton chicken ranch instead.

By December 1949, Menagh had sort of changed his mind again. He bought the controlling interest in a drive-in project north of Brighton, joining Lem Lee, Paul Rothman, and R. C. Otwell. The following March, Atlas Theatres, which owned the indoor Rex in Brighton, bought out the last three investors just weeks before the Kar-Vu opened.

The Kar-Vu's opening soon ad as it appeared in the *Brighton Blade*.

This grand opening photo "by Picken" ran on the front page of the *Brighton Blade* a couple of days after the Kar-Vu opened. Photo courtesy of the Brighton City Museum.

The narrow, long Kar-Vu sat just across then-US 85 and the railroad tracks from Brighton, northwest of town. Its wide concession-projection building was just three ramps away from the northeast-pointing screen.

In the summer of 1953, Menagh bought out Atlas's share of the Kar-Vu, then sold the drive-in a year and a half later to Sam Feinstein and Arlie Beery. After eight seasons, Feinstein sold it in early 1963 to Leonard Steele, operator of the Mile Hi Drive-In in Lead SD. Steele was the Kar-Vu's longest owner, selling it in February 1976 to Aldage Prevost, who ran the indoor Brighton Twin theaters.

The Kar-Vu's final season was in 1980. The May 1981 issue of *Boxoffice* reported, "One of the oldest drive-in theatres in the Denver metropolitan area, the Kar-Vu Drive In located in Brighton, Colorado, has ceased operation and is being dismantled."

Broomfield

Broomfield is more than a city; it's also the most recently created county in the United States. It held fewer than 8000 residents when its drive-in was born, but thanks in part to several annexations, it grew to over 35,000 by 1998. Thanks to that extra land, it was part of four other counties by then, so it convinced the state's voters to make the city a county as well. More than 70,000 live there today.

Nor-West Drive-In

Opened: March 23, 1967

Closed: 1996

Capacity: 600 cars

Leonard Steele, who was operating Brighton's Kar-Vu, and Stanley Sommers opened the Nor-West (sometimes spelled Nor'West or just Norwest) in the spring of 1967 at 120th Avenue and Perry Street. It was laid out much like other 1960s-vintage drive-ins, with a double-line cafeteria setup in the concession area. Steele said he

The Nor-West's screen stayed intact for years after the $600,000 drive-in closed. Photo by Kenneth James Mitchell.

hoped to expand the drive-in beyond its initial 600-car capacity as needed.

Before the 1969 season, Boulder-based Highland Theatres took over the Nor-West, then held it for a few years. Commonwealth bought the former Highland theaters in 1978, and the following year, it took over

The Nor-West's grand opening ad in the *Denver Post* used an apostrophe, not a hyphen, in its name.

operating the Wolfberg drive-ins, so the Nor-West finally got merged into the local Compass chain with the East, West, North, and South.

The Nor-West stayed in the Compass ad group into the late 1980s. Bill Holshue, former manager of the Lake Shore and owner of the 88, bought it before the decade was out. Holshue ran it until it closed in 1996. Mountain States Baptist Church bought the land, and a Broomfield man held a flea market there for one weekend before the city revoked his permit. Today the site is still undeveloped, with the ramps, concession building, and tower support bases still in place.

Brush

The city of Brush was named after cattle pioneer Jared Brush. He never actually lived in town, but he used to visit. Jared served four years as Colorado's lieutenant governor, and he lived in Greeley, where he helped start what became the University of Northern Colorado. In 1978, the city I will continue to refer to as Brush officially changed its name to "Brush!," with an exclamation point, to reflect its "can do attitude."

Brush Drive-In

Opened: July 1, 1951

Closed: Sept. 28, 1957

Capacity: 350 cars

Jacob "Jake" Bauer must have had some success when he built his first drive-in in 1950, in his home town of Fort Morgan. The next spring he got to work on a second just east of nearby Brush. Bauer logically named it the Brush Drive-In, and opened it on July 1, 1951. Three days later, a severe wind blew down the screen. About $2000 in repairs later, the Brush reopened on July 12.

John Roberts, who owned indoor theaters in Brush and Fort Morgan, bought both of Bauer's drive-ins in January 1952. William Ashton, who managed the indoor Emerson in Brush, became the seasonal manager of the Brush.

The winds returned in February 1953. In a scene that reminded locals of the Dust Bowl, dead branches and dust covered Brush's streets. The wind blew down the drive-in screen, flattened its fences, and smashed its neon lights. Ashton repaired the damage in time for the start of the drive-in season.

The *Brush News-Tribune* mentioned a silly incident in June 1954. Three teenage girls hid themselves in a car while two others paid at the box office. The punchline was that they went to all this trouble on a night when the Brush was charging $1 per carload.

The Brush was east of Beaver Creek, as seen in this USGS photo taken Sept. 26, 1953.

In early 1957, Roberts announced that neither the Emerson nor the Brush would open again, but Ashton worked out a lease and was announced as the new owner by late March. There followed one more summer season, from June 2 through Sept. 28, with the Emerson open only for Saturday matinees.

Brush DRIVE-IN Theater

Now Open!

ONE MILE EAST ON HIGHWAY 6

The Brush's ads were plain. This season opener ad in the *Brush News-Tribune* was the closest it got to a logo.

In April 1958, the Emerson reopened under new management, and the drive-in was officially abandoned. In July, Roberts sold its fences and poles, and in August, Ashton moved his family to New Mexico.

A correspondent at CinemaTreasures.org reported that when Joe Machetta bought the Emerson, he also tried to buy the Brush, "but the owner refused to sell it to him on moral principal since the drive-in was supposedly constructed in a bad location … the wind constantly blew sand and other debris around." From what I've read, he was probably right.

Buena Vista

Unlike the Spanish pronunciation, the correct way to say this town's name is "BEW-na Vista." Its founders knew in 1879 that the phrase meant "beautiful view," and one of them, Alsina Deerhammer, suggested it should take the first syllable of that English word, "beautiful." The town later named Alsina Street, two blocks west of US 24, for Mrs. Deerhammer.

Despite its location almost in the middle of nowhere, or maybe because of it, the Comanche sign and screen are magnets for any photographers passing by. 1997 photo by the author.

Comanche Drive-In

Opened: July 13, 1967

~~**Closed:**~~ active!

Capacity: 210 cars

John Lewis Groy grew up in a movie theater family; his father Lewis and uncle Ben built a drive-in in Salida in 1950. Later that year, he moved his family (including baby John D. Groy) to nearby Buena Vista, where he leased the indoor Pine Theater. In the spring of 1951, Groy had trouble renewing the Pine lease, so he built his own indoor theater, the Pearl, named for his wife.

In 1966, Groy picked a spot three miles west of downtown on the highway leading to Cottonwood Pass and began building his own drive-in. According to local newspapers and the Colorado Historical Society, the

This picture shows everything but the sign — the Comanche screen, trailer, snack bar, projection booth, and glorious mountains in back. © Depositphotos / steveheap

drive-in opened in July 1967. The first mention in *Boxoffice* was in October 1967 when it wrote, "John Groy has opened his new Comanche Drive-In."

The Comanche stayed in the family from that day forward. Its attendance dropped in the 1970s with the closing of the Climax Molybdenum mine about an hour's drive north. John D. and his wife Barbara eventually took over the Comanche, the Pearl, and the local coin laundry, keeping them all shuffling forward. A lightning strike fried the last of the in-car speakers in 2002, so the drive-in switched to radio sound. And there were a couple of years when, with family health issues, there were too many businesses to juggle, so the Comanche stayed temporarily dark.

John Lewis Groy passed away in April 2019, but the drive-in he built has switched to digital projection and continues to entertain audiences. In May 2020, it hosted the Buena Vista High School graduation. The Comanche remains the permanent-screen drive-in with the highest elevation anywhere, 7995 feet, and its setting at the foot of the Collegiate Peaks makes it a great place to visit.

Burlington

Burlington was the first taste of Colorado for me, as it is for many visitors driving in along I-70 from points east. Thousands of newcomers stop at the official Colorado Welcome Center there. During the summer, more of them should take advantage of the adjacent Old Town Museum, or they should check out the Kit Carson County Carousel on the north side of town.

Burlington Drive-In

Opened: May? 1976

Closed: Aug. 4, 1985

Capacity: 250 cars?

James Edmundson was about to turn 50 when he created what became the last drive-in built in Colorado during the 20th Century. Despite how recently it operated, most of its details already seem lost to history.

It probably opened in April or May 1976. The site of the Burlington Drive-In, about three miles east of town, was untouched pasture land in USGS aerial photos from June 1975, but the drive-in was complete by June 1976. The *Burlington Record* printed a tiny note on Page 2 of its May 6, 1976 issue, reporting that "Burlington's new Drive-In Theatre, owned and operated by Edmundson Theatres, is now open for business." The drive-in ran its first ad in that issue, not mentioning a grand opening.

The Burlington's final ad in the *Record* was Aug. 1, 1985, announcing that it would close for the season after Aug. 4, an unusually early closing. With video stores opening in town, it's easy to suspect that reduced attendance may have killed the drive-in.

This wasn't Edmundson's only theater; he operated several, indoor and drive-ins, mostly in western Kansas. He was a retired postmaster, married for over 50 years, and he passed away in Colby KS in 2008.

The Burlington's final ad in the *Burlington Record*.

Frankly, we're missing a lot of information about the Burlington. No ground-level photo. No description of its sign, if any. No reported capacity; from the aerial photo, showing an area of about 170,000 square feet, I'd guess around 200-250 cars. If you know more about it, please email mkilgore@carload.com.

Intermission: Common Denominators

Looking through all the details of the dozens of drive-in stories to be told in this book, there are some anecdotes that come so often that I rarely mention them:

1. Some patrons snuck into the drive-in without paying, often hidden in car trunks. In the old days when owners kept most of their ticket money, that was more of a big deal. Today, I'd think they'd almost welcome anyone interested in buying snacks. (See the Drive-In Economics section of the Brief History of Drive-Ins chapter.)

2. Some couples lost interest in the movie and became more enthusiastic about being with each other. Some of those couples later became parents. Let's leave it at that.

3. Thieves held up drive-ins and broke into their safes. A box office would build up a lot of cash on

The Star in Monte Vista has one of the few remaining drive-in theater playgrounds. 2006 photo © Captus Lumen Photography, used by permission.

weekends, and it was so easy to drive up, complete your transaction, then leave. It was also one of the few ways for a drive-in to get mentioned in local newspapers.

4. In the mid-1950s, pretty much every pre-existing drive-in widened its screen to accommodate wide-screen movies.

5. In those innocent days of low litigation, back when childhood injuries were seen as a rite of passage, drive-ins sported playgrounds. Some of them got elaborate with Ferris wheels and miniature trains. More often they were just long slides, seesaws and spinners, machined out of steel and bolted into the ground.

6. On Sunday mornings, many drive-ins hosted religious services. This happened a lot on Easter.

7. In the 1960s and later, many drive-ins added weekend flea markets.

So when I don't call out one of items on this list for a particular drive-in, it probably happened there anyway.

Cañon City

There aren't very many US cities with a tilde in the official name. Cañon City has had one since 1994. It was founded around 1860, and in 1868 Colorado offered Cañon City its choice of the state penitentiary or the state university. According to the *WPA Guide to Colorado*, "it chose the former because it was an established institution and seemed likely to be the better attended;" Boulder picked up the leftover University of Colorado.

Sunset Drive-In

Opened: Aug. 4, 1949

Closed: 1990

Capacity: 275 cars

George McCormick, who owned the indoor Skyline in town and a few more theaters elsewhere, built the Sunset 2½ miles east of Cañon City on US 50 in the summer of 1949. In 1953, his brother Harold quit his job with Intermountain Theatres to help run the Skyline and George's other theaters.

The Sunset's kitchen included one of Cañon City's first microwave ovens, which produced some of the city's first pizzas. Before the 1957 season, the McCormicks replaced the Sunset's screen. The new one was over 60 feet

Harold McCormick stands behind the Sunset's back row in this photo by George McCormick.

high and had almost double the old screen's surface area, and this one was covered with reflective MancoVision.

Both brothers were also active in politics. George was a city council member, and Harold was first elected to the Colorado House of Representatives in 1961. He served a total of 28 years in the state House and Senate.

Tragedy struck on July 12, 1969. George, an avid pilot, was flying the director and cameraman of the movie *Barquero* over one of the on-location sets near Cañon City. A wing touched the ground, and the plane cartwheeled into a crash. The cameraman was thrown free and survived, but the other two were trapped in the wreckage. George was killed almost instantly. The director, Robert Spaar, died of his injuries a month later.

Harold and his wife Jeanne continued to run the theaters while he periodically commuted to Denver for legislative work and to pick up new movies to show. Jeanne would run the Sunset Monday through Thursday. Harold would drive back on Friday afternoons to run the place through the last show Sunday night, then get back

You can see glimpses of the playground equipment at the base of the Sunset's wide screen. Photo by George McCormick.

on the highway early Monday morning to return to the capitol.

In 1976, Commonwealth Theatres leased the Sunset, and at the end of the season said they were sprucing it up a bit. Meanwhile Harold was the driving force behind the creation of the Colorado Motion Picture and Television Commission, the first of its kind in the US. The drive-in finally closed after the 1990 season and was dismantled the following year. There's a car dealership there today.

Castle Rock

If you ever visit Castle Rock, you won't have to guess at the source of its name. The stark, rocky butte in the center of town looms over the rest of town. In 1936, Works Progress Administration men built a star at the top of the butte. The star has lit up for the holiday season every year since 1945.

SHOWS START AT DUSK

EAST OF THE ROCK
ON COLO. HWY. 86

Phone 688-9646
Adults $1.00
Children 50c

CASTLE ROCK
Outdoor Cinema

I love to see a good logo in a drive-in newspaper ad. The 47 had mostly plain ads, but the tops of the Castle Rock Outdoor Cinema's ads were striking and effective.

47 / Outdoor Cinema / Castle Rock Drive-In

Opened: Aug. 12, 1956

Closed: 1976

Capacity: 200 cars

As James Petersen was building it, he ran a name-the-drive-in contest in the *Douglas County News*. The winning entry was "47," then part of the number of every license plate issued in Douglas County; Petersen thought it would show that he wanted to serve patrons from the entire region. It's rare for any drive-in to be named a number other than the highway it's on, except for a few named "70" for higher-definition 70mm projectors.

Peterson's builders reused six 50-foot, 12-inch think poles, former power wire supports for the Denver Trolley Company, to support the 47's screen. They attached corrugated metal to form the screen, swabbed with vinegar so paint would adhere to it. Half of the screen went up earlier, and workers hoisted the second half into place while early Grand Opening arrivals watched. That was good enough to start the show; the two halves were connected a few days later.

The little 47, which ran relatively short seasons every year, went through several name changes. In 1967, it started as the C. R. Drive-In, but was the Castle Rock 47 Drive-In by the end of the year. Then in 1969, Richard Pedersen, Bob Olds, and Bill Pence leased it and changed the name to the Castle Rock Cinema. By 1973, it advertised as the Castle Rock Outdoor Cinema, and it finally switched to Castle Rock Drive-In. After the 1976 season, the city approved redevelopment plans for the site, and the screen was dismantled in August 1977.

Center

The town of Center straddles Rio Grande and Saguache counties, about in the center of the San Luis Valley. Its population has stayed around 2000 for the past 80 years, though its businesses attract farmers from all directions in the region.

Frontier Drive-In

Opened: May 14, 1955

Closed: 1984?

Capacity: 320 cars

The Frontier held a free-admission Grand Opening, advertising in the *Monte Vista Journal* that it was "eleven miles north of Monte Vista on the Gunbarrel," the locals' name for US 285, which has no curves in that stretch. From the start, it had a wide 80x44-foot screen. The Frontier was owned by Herbert and Theta Gumper, who also owned the Center Theatre, the La Jara Theatre, and the Round-Up Drive-In in La Jara.

The Frontier's marquee, and most of the rest of it for that matter, were still well preserved by the near-desert plateau of the San Juan Valley. 1999 photo by the author.

Gumper passed away during a fishing trip in July 1964. The following season, local grocer Roger Skeff took over the Frontier as well as the indoor Center theater. Skeff, who sometimes ran Spanish language features during the week, was later elected to the board of directors of Associated Grocers. Ed Bohn took over the Frontier before the 1975 season, one reference started calling it the "New Frontier," and that's where my information trails off. The drive-in's last appearance in the *Motion Picture Almanac* was the 1984 edition, which suggests that it closed for good a year or two earlier.

The dry air has helped preserve the Frontier's screen and sign. In 2018, a Denver company said it planned to restore them as part of a larger community center and corporate retreat. In late 2019, it had hoped to finish its work by summer 2020.

Colorado Springs

Pikes Peak dominates the Colorado Springs skyline, and it figures in a lot of its history. Colorado City was founded during the Pikes Peak Gold Rush of 1859 and was briefly the capital of the Colorado Territory. General William Palmer founded Colorado Springs as a resort town, with Pikes Peak as a big attraction, and annexed Colorado City. Although there were more drive-ins in the Denver metropolitan area, Colorado Springs held the most of any single city.

8th Street Drive-In

Opened: May 5, 1950

Closed: Sept. 28, 1984

Capacity: 700 cars

Westland Theatres owned the Chief and Peak indoor theaters in Colorado Springs when it began work on the city's second drive-in, located on 15 acres atop a hill at Brookside Avenue and 8th Street. That location may have helped it; the 8th Street was less than two miles from downtown compared to the Starlight over four miles east.

When the 8th Street opened, it had a grassed-in playground, lighted speaker poles, and attendants to wipe windshields and fix flat tires. Probably looking for another competitive advantage, it promoted its "moonlight" lamps, mounted on three 25-foot poles in the back and controlled by dimmers. The local *Gazette-Telegraph* wrote that they were "the first to be installed west of the Mississippi River and are the latest type developed for drive-in theatres."

The original, wider version of this 1955 photo of the 8th Street, with more mountains fading into the haze, is even more magnificent. Too bad this page is too narrow to do it justice. Photograph by Myron Wood, © Pikes Peak Library District, 002-2831. Look up the original at ppld.org.

In 1952, the 8th Street added an "elephant slide" to the playground, and *Boxoffice* wrote that the manager of the Chief helped the drive-in's manager test it.

The drive-in led a quiet, corporate-owned life. In April 1984, Westland sold the 8th Street to local real estate developers but kept it going for one last season. Its final show on Sept. 28 that year was mentioned in newspapers across the country because its film that night was *The Last Picture Show*.

Aircadia Drive-In

Opened: April 8, 1955

Closed: Sept. 3, 1995

Capacity: 800 cars

When Westland built its second drive-in, it was on US 24 just east of the Colorado Springs city limits, two miles closer to town than the still-remote Starlight. They

This photo, reportedly taken in 1961, shows just how remote these two drive-ins were to Colorado Springs. Looking west toward the mountains, the Aircadia is at the edge of town, south (left) of the highway near the center of the photo. The Starlight, built 13 years earlier, still sits alone at the lower right. Photograph by Stewarts Commercial Photographers, © Pikes Peak Library District, 013-11012.

pulled out all the stops, calling it "The theatre of tomorrow – today!" Westland brought over their most experienced manager and projection from the 8th Street to take over its new showcase.

The Aircadia's massive 96x75-foot screen faced west 500 feet from the second-floor projection booth. On the ground floor, a patio stretched to the front. The fenced-off "Fairyland" playground behind the building entertained kids before the show. The floor of the cafeteria-style concession room was tiled in green and yellow.

Any number of drive-ins hosted church services, but the Aircadia took it a step further with "Cowboy Church." The First Methodist Church started it on Aug. 13, 1967 to serve guests in town for the Pikes Peak or Bust Rodeo. Men on horseback would use their hats to gather contributions from the congregation in their cars. As late as 1978, the First United Methodist Church was continuing Cowboy Church as a three-month summer tradition. Ushers were still on horseback.

In general, the Aircadia's years were uneventful while corporate ownership kept changing. Commonwealth Theatres bought Westland's theaters in early 1985, then United Artists bought a big chunk of Commonwealth in 1988. But at the end of the drive-in's life, it was Westland that sold the land, so I guess they always owned it.

In early 1995, Walmart announced that it was going to build on the site, prompting one last season of nostalgia for the last drive-in in Colorado Springs. On the Aircadia's final night, cars were backed up two blocks on East Platte Avenue to get in. Today, that Walmart is still there.

Falcon Drive-In

Opened: Aug. 2, 1969

Closed: Nov. 1, 1983

Capacity: 614 cars

The Falcon was a great example of the 1960s-era modern drive-in located in burgeoning suburbs. Westland Theatres, which already owned most of the other local drive-ins, built it a mile east of Academy

Boulevard on Austin Bluffs Parkway. It had a steel screen tower supporting a wide 80x40-foot screen, a narrow steel refreshment / projection building with a playground behind it, and a lovely sign with Falcon written in script.

The Falcon's movies reflected how drive-in movies in general changed over the years. Its first movie was the John Wayne western *The Sons of Katie Elder*. Its final program at the end of the 1983 season was *The Dorm That Dripped Blood* and *The Day After Halloween*.

After the Falcon led a quiet 15 seasons, Westland sold it to a developer for $2 million in April 1984. Clayton Cheever, a company vice-president, later told the *Gazette* that they hadn't been shopping their drive-ins. "People just came to us and offered us some staggering amounts of money," he said. "When the first one sold, that evidently let the word out that you could buy them if the dollars were right."

Northside Drive-In

Opened: May 26, 1950

Closed: Oct. 3, 1961

Capacity: 400 cars

Paul Rothman and Cy Lee, who had built the Starlight east of Colorado Springs, picked a site on the north side of town for their second local drive-in. A greyhound racing track had opened in July 1949; by October, construction had begun of the Northside one block west of the track. The

Although it was on Cascade Avenue west of Nevada Avenue, the Northside often described its location as near the greyhound racing track.

The Northside's single-story projection booth and the box office are easy to see in this 1952 photo, but where was the marquee? Probably on Nevada Avenue one block east. Photograph by Stewarts Commercial Photographers, © Pikes Peak Library District, 013-2074.

Grand Opening ad the following spring promised roses for the ladies and picnic tables for all to enjoy.

Rothman must have been busy with his many drive-ins and projects at that point. In September 1950, he leased the Northside to local real estate man D. C. Trester, effective Spring 1951. But in June 1951, Rothman leased the drive-in to Texas theater operator W. Lloyd Perry.

Before the 1952 season, Kelso and Lem Lee bought out enough of Rothman's interest to gain a controlling share. They said that they would add a 350-seat auditorium in 1953 so the Northside could operate all winter. I don't think that ever happened.

In December 1954, Westland Theatres, which ran most of Colorado Springs's other drive-ins, took over operation of the Northside from Lee Theatres. After Westland built the larger Aircadia the next year and added more local drive-ins in the 1950s, the Northside faded in importance. Its final movie played at the end of the 1961 season. Mobile home parks occupy the site today.

Sky-Vue Drive-In

Opened: July 28, 1955

Closed: Oct. 4, 1983

Capacity: 380 cars

I'll admit it. I don't have a whole lot of information about the Sky-Vue, sometimes written as the Sky View. It was a narrow drive-in, with a wide screen facing the northeast. It was on the west side of town on 21st Street, seven blocks south of Colorado Avenue. It opened fairly late in the 1955 season.

Who built it? The *Motion Picture Almanac* said that R. N. Cullen was in charge at the end of 1956. But in late 1957, *Boxoffice* reported that Florida man Charles Sutton had sold or leased (its accounts varied) the Sky-Vue to Westland Theatres, and that Sutton was the one who built it.

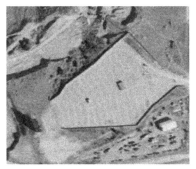

At the time, Westland already ran other drive-ins nearby — the 8th Street, Aircadia, Northside, Starlight, and maybe the Vista Vue. So the Sky Vue settled in to a quarter century of quiet corporate-owned life.

In April 1984, Westland president Neal Lloyd told the

The Sky-Vue's narrow viewing field matched the apartment complex that took its place.
© Historicaerials.com, used by permission

Colorado Springs *Gazette* that he had no plans to sell the Sky Vue, but it didn't reopen that year. Construction on the site began the following January. Today, the Altamira Apartments occupy that space, surrounded by Skyview Lane.

Starlight / Starlite Drive-In

Opened: June 30, 1948

Closed: Nov. 21, 1964

Capacity: 1000 cars

Cy Lee and Paul Rothman bought the official "Park-In" franchise for Colorado Springs in early 1948, and they went right to work building the Starlight a few miles east of town. That's the way it was spelled in its Grand Opening ads and on the neon sign at its entrance.

The new Starlight was only the fourth drive-in to open in Colorado. Its lot held 450 cars facing "100 miles of mountain range" behind its northeast-facing screen, built of 54 tons of steel. The "Snack Shack" in the middle of the viewing area featured all the usual theater food plus a free bottle warmer for babies.

There are occasional stories elsewhere of busloads of patrons taking advantage of "Carload" priced nights, but the Starlight recorded the only anecdote I've read of a per-person busload. During that first season, a local boys' home brought 36 kids and paid $21.40 to see a movie. Lee and Rothman escorted the bus to a stall, hooked up four speakers, and everyone was happy.

Business must have been good, because the owners opened the Northside less than two years after the Starlight's opener. After the 1950 season, ownership shifted. Rothman bought out Lee's share of both drive-ins, leased the Northside to a real estate man, and

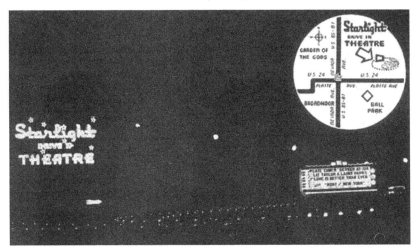

This was the front of an undated promotional postcard for the Starlight. It was probably printed in 1952 or soon after, because the back mentioned its 1000-car capacity and specified two-cent postage, which was valid 1952-58.

concentrated on improving the Starlight. On maybe that was the "Starlite," since that was the way it began to be spelled in ads and stories in the local newspaper.

In 1951, the Starlite added a 30-foot, gasoline-powered train to the playground below the screen. Rothman said, "It was designed so that Mom and Dad can ride along with the little folks." In 1952, Rothman expanded the viewing field to hold 1000 cars.

Westland Theatres, which owned the 8th Street and a couple of downtown indoor theaters, bought the Starlite after the 1954 season. The drive-in quietly spent a decade as part of Westland's growing chain, then closed after the 1964 season. That heavy screen stayed up for another year before workers dismantled it in December 1965.

Vista View Drive-In

Listed under the city of Fountain.

Commerce City

One of its first features in present-day Commerce City was Riverside Cemetery at 52nd Ave. and Brighton Blvd, an omen of failed, pre-Commerce City towns to come. Derby, once a Burlington Railroad station, Born: 1889, Died 1891. Irondale, named for a foundry, Born: 1889, Incorporated: 1924, Died: 1930s. Adams City, failed candidate for county seat: Born 1903, Died 1922. The string was broken when Commerce Town incorporated in 1952, changed its name to Commerce City a decade later, and kept on growing.

East 88th Avenue / 88 Drive-In

Opened: Aug. 12, 1971

~~**Closed:**~~ active!

Capacity: 500 cars

The East 88th Avenue opened in August 1971, less than a mile east of I-76, after a neighborhood petition drive in support of a zoning variance helped it become possible. It was built by Paul Cory, who owned the Starlite Drive-In in Sterling among other theaters. That first season passed quietly, though reportedly unprofitably.

At the beginning of the 1972 season, the drive-in switched to X-rated movies. The previously supportive neighbors were very unhappy about the change. Motorists were distracted by the explicit events on-screen. So many children watched from the roof of the school across the street that the school district built a fence to keep the kids off. The drive-in asked the county for permission to build its own 30-foot fence, but was denied. The drive-in decided to erect poles to support a light screen to block

The "east" was still hanging in there on the drive-in's sign in this 1997 photo by the author.

the view, but the county objected, getting the courts to hold Cory in contempt until the poles came down. In November, Cory told the court that he'd sold the East 88th Street to Olympic Drive-In Theatres of St. Louis. The drive-in filed appeals, bought some car heaters, and settled in to wait out the winter.

On the afternoon of Feb. 11, 1973, a bomb went off in the concession stand, blowing a 12-inch hole in the wall and causing about $1500 damage. Earlier, some guy had assaulted manager Michael Middleton in a grocery store; the suspect was booked and released on bail.

In early March, a court issued an injunction to shut down the drive-in, but that failed because it used the wrong address. (It said 8700 Rosemary St. instead of the accurate 8780 Rosemary.) The East 88th Avenue reopened for the season, only to face an attempted blockade by neighbors' cars. Finally, later in the month, another court landed a successful injunction using a different tack, shutting down the drive-in until it had installed curbs, sidewalks and such as promised in its original zoning variance, to the satisfaction of the county. Which was not in the mood to be satisfied.

Somehow in May, the East 88th Avenue must have reached a settlement. The injunctions were waived as the owners promised to lay off the X-rated stuff. Projectionist Paul Rabe was installed as the new manager.

In April 1974, EMW Management of Houston sold the East 88th Avenue to Steve Eisner of Scottsdale AZ. The drive-in was listed for sale in a January 1976 classified ad in *Boxoffice*, and that's about when Bill Holshue, longtime manager of the Lake Shore Drive-In in Lakewood, bought it. The rest is much quieter history.

Perhaps looking to make a clean break, Holshue emphasized the 88 in its newspaper ads. By 1977, it was simply the 88; even the drive-in's sign eventually dropped the "east." Around the turn of the millenium, Bill and Margaret Holshue passed the drive-in down to their daughter Susan Kochevar, who still runs it today.

Cortez

Cortez was founded in 1887 by the Montezuma Valley Water Company to house the hundreds of workers who built an elaborate system of tunnels and ditches to provide irrigation from the Dolores River. The following decades were punctuated by booms and busts, from farms to orchards to uranium to oil. Tourism, partly from nearby Mesa Verde National Park, has been a steadier source of income.

Arroyo / Arroya Drive-In

Opened: Sept. 3, 1950

Closed: 1988?

Capacity: 300 cars

Theatre magnate John Survant, owner of the indoor An Le in Cortez, commissioned the Arroyo Drive-In on US 160 in the northwest part of town. The drive-in might have been named for the steep hills on the other side of the highway, as if they had been carved by a fast-moving stream. Or maybe he just liked the name; it was misspelled often enough.

The Arroyo was supposed to open in the summer of 1950, but on Aug. 5 that year, a cable snapped as workers were lifting the wooden screen tower into place, with the tower's fall "splintering" the pre-fab structure. A grand-opening front-page story in the *Cortez Sentinel* two weeks later spelled the name "Arroya," as did a huge Grand Opening ad. The following week included a smaller ad apologizing for that delay and getting the grand opening date right. Two weeks after opening, the ad spelling was finally changed to "Arroyo".

Survant died in Montana after a fall in June 1951. Terenzio and Anna

In its true grand opening ad, the Arroyo still wasn't sure how it wanted to be spelled.

Gai bought a half-interest in 1952, then bought the rest from the Survant estate in early 1953. Two years later, Terenzio spelled it again as the "Arroya" in a statewide supplement ad in the *Eagle Valley Enterprise* and in many of its early 1960s ads in the *Sentinel*.

In 1967, daughter Margory Gai sold the Arroyo along with Cortez's indoor theaters to Allen Theatres, started by Lane Allen of Farmington. Mark Wolfe wrote in *Silver Screens Under Starry Skies* that while Allen owned it, admission to the Arroyo was always by the carload. (His photo accompanying that article showed the faded sign spelled Arroyo.) In 1988, hearing that it would cost $7500 to repaint the screen, Allen closed the Arroyo. Today, Allen Theatres still operates the indoor Fiesta Theatre in Cortez.

Independent Drive-In

Opened: July 31, 1949

Closed: October 2, 1949

Capacity: 75 cars

The aptly named Independent was Cortez's first drive-in theater. It lasted just nine weeks, but it paved the way for those that would follow. As far as I can tell, this is the first time the Independent has been mentioned in print for 70 years.

Almost all of the story of the Independent comes from the pages of the *Cortez Sentinel*. The front of its July 28, 1949 issue proclaimed the coming opening of the town's first drive-in on US 160 in northwest Cortez "just south of Chub's Cabinet Shop," although its precise location was never revealed. Philip Belt, an 18-year-old who lived in nearby Dolores, owned and operated the

Independent. The makeshift drive-in had room for about 75 cars, held two shows per night except Fridays, and relied on "three outdoor amplifiers" for movie sound.

In the Independent's ad three weeks later, Belt wrote, "We are very sorry if our little Drive-In seems kind of "shacky" … but our original plan was to build a small outfit, and if people came and showed interest, we will build a 35 mm regular drive-in next spring. However, we haven't done well enough to make us feel that an $18,000 drive-in would pay."

On Aug. 25, the front-page news was that the Independent was installing 40 individual speakers on poles, one for each pair of cars. Belt said the previous loudspeaker system had always been temporary until the smaller speakers arrived.

An ominous note in the Sept. 29 ad read, "We are not responsible for any accident, or otherwise contracted, from cutting our speaker lines as we are leaving 110 volts current in said lines to prevent them being mutilated." The *Sentinel* wrote that "several times in the past (Belt) has found wires leading to the individual speakers clipped, making one or more of the speakers inoperable. He believes the damage

Although there weren't that many of them, ads for the Independent were usually verbose, providing some of the best clues to its history.

has been done by kids. The electricity had formerly been cut off when the theater was not in operation."

There were no reports of shocked vandals, and just one week later, the Independent's ad said that it would suspend operations because of cooler weather. "Thanks for coming; we have enjoyed meeting you."

Boxoffice followed with its only mention of the Independent, noting in its Nov. 12 issue that it had closed for the season. That drive-in never reopened, but Belt stayed in the movie business nearby. When the Arroyo opened the following year, possibly on the same site, Belt worked there as a projectionist. He later worked at the indoor Cortez Theatre for a few years, and in early 1956, he bought the indoor Mancos Theatre in nearby Mancos. On Oct. 5, 1957, *Boxoffice* reported that Belt was "completing a 250-car drive-in theatre" there, but I haven't found anything that corroborates that note. Eventually Belt started Phil's TV Service in Cortez, then managed the Radio Shack there. He passed away in 2015 at the age of 83.

Tsaya Drive-In

Opened: April 21, 1955

Closed: 1966?

Capacity: 320 cars

Probably inspired by the Arroyo's success, Ralph Tanner, Raymond Taylor, and George Armstrong built the Tsaya, named for the Navajo word for the community that became Cortez. Its literal meaning is "water under the rock," an apt description of nearby Mitchell Springs.

In the southwest part of town on then-US 666, the Tsaya had a wide 42x84-foot screen mounted on a 65-foot tower. Orange-painted speakers indicated the poles which also had in-car heaters.

The Tsaya's owners added a roller skating rink in 1959 and a six-bed trampoline center in 1960, but soon sold out to the owners of the Arroyo Drive-In. By May 1967, Margory Gai had closed the Tsaya.

The *Motion Picture Almanac*, which published its national drive-in list pretty much on autopilot from 1967-1976, made an exception in its 1969 edition when it dropped the Tsaya. The screen was torn down in the 1970s.

Was this ever the sign for the Tsaya Drive-In? I'd like to think so, but it was probably always for the nearby Tsaya Trading Post. 1991 photo by John Margolies.

Craig

Craig was founded by William Tucker and incorporated as a city in 1908. When Moffat County was split off from Routt County in 1911, Craig became the county seat. When in town, check out the Museum of Northwest Colorado, housed in the former Colorado State Armory.

Sunset / Romantic / Motor View Drive-In

Opened: Aug. 6, 1954

Closed: 1991?

Capacity: 280

Schumour Theatres, which owned the indoor theaters in Craig, built well when it constructed the

The broad, sturdy screen tower of the Romantic, or perhaps the Motor View, in 1980. Photo by John Margolies.

Sunset Drive-In on US 40 about a mile east of town. Its screen required a boxcar of 2-by-6 wood, attached to a steel frame welded by a blacksmith. The owners later covered the wooden screen with more reflective corrugated steel.

The drive-in was ready to open on Aug. 5, 1954, but a soaking rain turned the as-yet ungraveled ramps to mud. Opening Night was postponed to the 6th. Crowds responded to the novelty of the Sunset early on, but its high elevation and northern latitude kept seasons short. The Sunset closed in the late 1960s or early 1970s.

Wesley Webb and Stanley Dewsnup, who were running the theaters in Delta, took over the indoor West in Craig in early 1976. As part of the deal they also got the closed but intact drive-in, which they reopened as the Romantic that May.

I'm not sure whether Craig's drive-in closed again, but by the 1980s, it was advertising in the *Steamboat Pilot* as the Motor View. Those ads persisted until the early 1990s.

After the turn of the millennium, Craig city officials would occasionally grumble about Dewsnup and the undermaintained former drive-in screen, but there was nothing they could really do because the former Sunset was outside the city limits. Dewsnup once put on a fresh coat of paint and a "soon re-opening" sign, saying that he would switch to FM radio sound, but I don't believe it ever really reopened.

In late summer 2007, a gravel yard next door took control of the old drive-in site and burned down the concession/projection building while locals came by to pay their respects. In 2014, the Craig Chamber of Commerce began work on a mural for that remarkably durable screen tower. Today that mural reads, "Welcome to Moffat County".

Intermission: The Alexander Film Company

Colorado was home to one of the movie business's pioneers. At its peak, the Alexander Film Company produced over 160,000 feet of film per day and shipped it to thousands of theaters across the US and Canada.

It was started by two brothers. Julian Don Alexander was born in St. Louis in 1885; his brother Don Miller Alexander came along in 1893 in Chattanooga TN. After they were orphaned, their travels continued to Keokuk IA, where they lived with their grandparents. There the boys found an old French stereopticon and some colored comedy slides in their grandfather's attic. They built an

This 1950s postcard published for the Alexander Film Company gave an idea of the sprawl of its campus. On the back it read, "Greetings from the world's largest theatre and television film advertising studios!"

arc light, sewed bedsheets for a screen, and asked local merchants to buy advertising for their shows. Hanging the screen from their grandfather's store and projecting the images for anyone to see, the Alexanders created something a little bit like a drive-in theater.

Older brother J. Don (as he was always called) moved to Spokane WA to be a cameraman for Paramount. Don M. earned an engineering degree from Washington State University. Together, they started their own electrical shop in Spokane, J. Don as the salesman and Don M. as the guy to create whatever his brother sold. The story goes that one day in 1919, a client wanted to create a film ad to run at the local theater before the movie. Don M. whipped that up, and its success convinced them to do the same for other businesses.

Note that this all happened before commercial radio, not to mention TV. The Alexander brothers had invented video ads, which they called "advertising playlets."

The brothers did so well in Spokane that they decided to spread their business to clients and theaters across the country. They reasoned that a more central location would help, so they moved to Englewood CO. The flamboyant J. Don was also a pilot, and wanted to use 1920s airplanes to cover more territory and deliver films faster. When he couldn't get any manufacturers to build him enough planes for his fleet of salesmen, he turned to his brother to organize an airplane factory in Englewood. They created the Eaglerock, possibly the most popular plane of the 1920s.

As the company grew, the brothers looked to expand to a larger facility. Colorado Springs offered them a great deal on a large piece of land on the north side of town. They began erecting 10 buildings there in January 1928. On April 20, a spark from an electric fan hit an open pan of silver nitrate in the Englewood aircraft shop. The resulting horrific fire killed 11. Faced with the prospect of suspending operations while the investigation continued, the brothers roused their 350 employees before dawn on April 24 and began an impromptu one-day truck caravan to the new site. J. Don and Don M., along with three other plant supervisors, were charged with manslaughter as a result of the fire. They later pleaded guilty to "violating the state factory law," and paid fines of $200 each. The other charges were dropped.

This odd ad is from the June 21, 1952 issue of *Boxoffice*.

The Alexander Film Company settled in and expanded its campus. The site eventually included dozens of film stages and a full animation department. The Great Depression killed demand for their airplanes, but increased it for their movie ads. Most Americans continued to patronize their

Alexander Film Co. often used its home town's scenic beauty, as in this ad filmed at the Garden of the Gods.

local theaters, and merchants were more eager than ever to reach them. Don M. created his own form of color film process. The flamboyant J. Don brought prospective clients to Colorado Springs to tour the facilities; when he wasn't around, his cardboard cutout and tape-recorded voice would greet them.

In the 1940s and 1950s, television began eroding demand for theatrical ads as small local theaters withered away. To a large extent, the surge of drive-in theaters picked up the slack, since they needed intermission ads as well as those for local merchants. Alexander Film was a pioneer of the intermission "clock" counting down 10 minutes to the second movie of a typical double feature.

J. Don passed away in 1955. Don M. took over managing the company for a couple of years, but he didn't have his brother's flair; he retired as president in 1957. The Alexander Film Company continued making TV and movie ads through the 1960s. Before the 1960s were done, Alexander Film had morphed into a film reproduction and processing plant for Hollywood studios. Don M. died in 1971. The company limped along for decades, shedding buildings along the way. It was specializing in transferring film and video to digital when it closed for good in 2012.

Delta

The City of Delta, named for the delta where the Uncompahgre River flows north into the Gunnison River, incorporated in 1882. Its population during the last half of the 20th Century stayed around 4000, but it has doubled since the turn of the millennium. The magnificent indoor Egyptian Theatre there opened in 1928 and was where Charles "C. U." Yaeger invented Bank Night. The Egyptian remains open today.

Skylite / Big Sky Drive-In

Opened: May 10, 1949

Closed: 1986

Capacity: 400 cars

In March 1949, the *Delta County Independent* wrote that Max Story from Meeker had purchased 10 acres of land a half mile east of Delta to build a drive-in. The Skylite would be just the second one built on the Western Slope, almost two years after Grand Junction's Starlite opened.

By April, *Boxoffice* was reporting that Harry Baird and Edgar Jones, from Vernal UT, had joined Story's project. Ted Knox supplied the booth equipment and in-car speakers, and the Skylite opened on time on May 10.

Story managed the drive-in, and most early stories (no pun intended) called him the owner. Before the 1950 season, he renovated the Skylite, adding new lamp houses and resurfacing the ramps. Toward the end of that season, Story reopened the

SKYLITE

Drive-In Theatre
DELTA, COLORADO
"Come as you are in the Family Car"

Part of a 1949 newspaper ad. Didn't anyone notice they were using TV clipart to advertise a drive-in?

indoor Strand, running that in the months when the drive-in was closed.

In July 1951, Story sold his share of the Skylite to Jones. On Aug. 2, the Skylite shot off a large set of fireworks as part of Deltarado Days; hundreds of extra cars parked near the drive-in to watch the display.

By the mid-1950s, the guy running the Skylite was Jones's son-in-law, William Tagert. Most of the drive-in was outside the city limits, and Tagert repeatedly asked the city council if he could hook into the local electrical grid and stop paying a higher rate to the Delta-Montrose Rural Power Lines Association. F. M. Peterson, manager of the electric co-op, pointed out his group had spent almost $10,000 to run power lines to the Skylite. Peterson would soon build his own drive-in in nearby Hotchkiss.

In 1959, Tagert was running Delta's indoor Egyptian as well as the Skylite, and he somehow got the wife of the competing Tru-Vu Drive-In to sell him her interest. The next couple of years were a remarkable story of intertwined family and business feuding. I'll try to tell that story in the Tru-Vu's section of this book, coming up soon.

In the aftermath of the Delta drive-in war, Jones regained control of the Skylite. Tagert filed for divorce in October 1962, remarried in September 1963, and moved

The Big Sky's screen and sign are remarkably intact after over 30 years of inactivity, though there is little left of the rest of the drive-in. 2019 photo by the author.

to Aspen. After the 1963 season, Egyptian manager Tom Hardy bought the drive-in, remodeling it and renaming it the Big Sky.

In February 1968, Hardy crashed a light plane, which killed him and three friends. A few months later, Jeannie and Stanley Dewsnup of Santaquin UT saw in an ad in *Boxoffice* that Delta's theaters were for sale. They came to visit and bought them all.

The Dewsnups kept both of the formerly competing drive-ins operating, showing a lot of Spanish-language films at the Big Sky. After the oil shale bust of the 1980s, money drained out of Delta, so they decided to close one of the drive-ins. The Tru-Vu had less light pollution, so it survived.

The Big Sky is still there today, almost intact. The sign is badly faded, the screen has lost a small slice, and only a foundation marks where the projection building had been. Not far away, you can see the Tru-Vu's screen, and that's probably the biggest reason the Big Sky is unlikely to reopen.

Tru Vu Drive-In

Opened: March 11, 1955

~~Closed:~~ active!

Capacity: 400 cars

How many pages do I have left in this book? I might have to use all of them for the history of the Tru Vu, the timeless drive-in on the cover.

I have to first admit that I'm just a little fuzzy on the Tru Vu's origins. Max Story had returned to Delta after selling his interest in the Skylite a couple of years earlier, and he apparently went to work on building a competitor less than a mile away, right on state highway 92. The Jan. 29, 1955 issue of *Boxoffice* reported that Stanley and Ann Dixon had purchased Delta's "Motor-Vu" from Story. A month later, the magazine said the Dixons, "owners of the Motor-Vu Drive-In, Delta," were off on vacation. In between, a farm machinery auction in the Feb. 9 Grand Junction *Daily Sentinel* described its location as "just west of the Tru-Vu Drive-In".

The Tru Vu called its 1955 debut a "grand opening"in its first newspaper ad.

It's remarkable how little the Tru Vu changed in the 19 years between this book's cover photo and this 1998 photo by the author.

The Tru Vu announced its grand opening for March 11, 1955 in an ad in the *Delta County Independent*. Was that merely a season opener, because Story had opened it (or the Motor Vu) in 1954? The mostly reliable *Theatre Catalog* didn't include the Tru Vu or Motor Vu in its 1955-56 edition, so I'll have to guess that ad was for a true grand opening.

The ground gets firmer after that opener, though it quickly becomes rocky. The Gunnison River flooded in June 1957, turning the Tru Vu viewing field into a shallow lake. Just two months later, the Dixons sold the drive-in to Austrian immigrant Fred Chubka and his wife.

The following account of the next four years, which I will call the Delta Drive-In War until I can think of a better title for the eventual HBO mini-series, is all strictly based on reports from the *Daily Sentinel*. If any of these parties' estates want to tell different perspectives of these events, I'd be happy to add them to a special page at Carload.com and to the next edition of this book. Please don't sue me.

Within months of purchasing the Tru Vu, Fred and June Chubka encountered an odd pattern of vandalism. In January 1958, thorough mischief-makers destroyed the marquee, broke every window in the cashier's cage and the concession building, and whacked the projectors with hammers. In September, vandals ripped out 14 speakers plus 72 of the wires connecting other speakers to the sound system. In October, 26 more speakers and their wires went missing overnight.

Reports of vandalism cooled off in 1959, though there was a stranger turn. William Tagert, who owned the competing Skylite Drive-In, somehow persuaded June Chubka to sell him her share of the Tru Vu. Fred continued to run his drive-in, but that must have been odd.

Then came the fire that temporarily shut down the Tru Vu. In July 1960, a teenager familiar to the Tagerts set the blaze that gutted the two-story concession / projection building. Although the arsonist confessed and was convicted of the crime, I'm withholding all identifying details because the perpetrator was still a juvenile.

The Chubkas weren't the only theater family encountering oddly thorough vandalism. In January 1961, the screen at the indoor Egyptian, also owned by Tagert, was ripped and slashed, and its office was also ransacked, though nothing was missing.

In October 1961, the Chubkas sued the Tagerts for causing the fire, even though the arsonist claimed to have acted alone. At the trial, the Chubkas introduced evidence that June might have been mentally ill when she

Another angle of the Tru Vu sign. What's the name for the style for signs with those holes? The Valley in Fort Morgan had one like that. 1998 photo by the author.

sold her share to Tagert, which could not have been good for their marriage. That trial ended in a hung jury, and the Chubkas refiled the lawsuit to be heard in early 1962. After delays, on May 14, the date the second trial was to begin, the two parties reached an out-of-court settlement. On Aug. 20, June filed for divorce from Fred.

I never saw the details of the settlement of that lawsuit, but there was a hint in a note in the May 28, 1963 *Daily Sentinel* that mentioned that both Delta drive-ins had been burglarized. It said that a few things were missing at the Skylite but nothing was gone "from the unused Tru-Vu Theater. The break-ins were discovered this morning by the owner, Fred Chubka."

By August 1963, Egyptian manager Tom Hardy was also running the Tru Vu. Just one month later, the *Daily Sentinel* announced that the Tru Vu had reopened "under the new ownership of Police Chief Dan Morgan and James Hanson, both of Delta. The theater ... was sold through the district court to expedite property settlement in a divorce case".

One more time, I'm a bit fuzzy on how Morgan and Hanson came to sell the drive-in they bought just five years earlier, but the Tru Vu was definitely on the market when Jeannie and Stanley Dewsnup of Santaquin UT bought all of Delta's theaters in 1968. The Dewsnups later said that when they first walked into the Tru Vu's projection room, the walls were still black from the fire.

From all accounts, the Dewsnups became beloved in Delta. When it came to close one of their drive-ins, they chose the Tru Vu as the one to stay in operation. Stanley passed away in 2008, and Jeannie died in April 2019. James Lane and his family stepped in to run the drive-in only to get smacked by the craziness that is 2020. For now, the Tru Vu continues to entertain.

Denver

This might get a little confusing. Many drive-ins that you might think of as being in Denver, even some that were marked as "Denver" in old lists of drive-ins, were actually in Denver's suburbs. I'll include their names here, along with where you can find their full descriptions in this book.

88 Drive-In

Listed under Commerce City.

Arapahoe Drive-In

Listed under Greenwood Village.

Centennial Drive-In

Listed under the city of Littleton.

Cinderella Twin Drive-In

Listed under the city of Sheridan.

Denver Mart Drive-In

Opened: June 12, 2015

~~Closed:~~ active!

Capacity: 275 cars

Here's a short entry for a drive-in that hasn't been around very long. The folks at the Denver Mart, built in 1965 as a host for trade shows and such, realized in 2015 that their north parking lot could be transformed into a

The Denver Mart is little more than a flat parking lot and a large screen, which may prove that's all a drive-in really needs. 2017 photo by the author.

drive-in. They erected a 92x40-foot screen 20 feet high, with its back to I-25. Then they laid out the parking spaces, using fewer than they had originally hoped, and opened that summer.

Tickets for the Denver Mart Drive-In are available only online; since there are only about 275 parking spots, it's reassuring to be able to nail down one of them before leaving home. Its location at Washington Street and 58th Avenue is just east of I-25. The snack bar and rest rooms are inside the Denver Mart.

Trains run along the tracks just north of the drive-in a couple of times a night, and the flat parking lot lacks the retro appeal of drive-in ramps, but the Denver Mart is a great example of an inventive 21st-century ozoner.

East / East 70 Drive-In

Listed under the city of Aurora.

Evans Drive-In

Opened: Aug. 11, 1954

Closed: Jan. 10, 1982

Capacity: 592 cars plus 120 seats

R. L. "Mickey" Stanger, who had owned the indoor Windsor in Windsor CO, moved to Denver and partnered with Cecil Willars there to build the Evans Walk-In Drive-In on Evans Avenue just east of Federal Boulevard. It started with a 120-seat auditorium on the ground floor along with the concession stand and projection booth, but there were plans to turn it into a two-story building. The Evans squeezed 592 cars into its 7½-acre plot. It had been originally scheduled for a July 1 grand opening, but was delayed for weeks because of a construction strike, the first of many labor disputes.

Thanks to that indoor auditorium and 100 in-car heaters, the Evans stayed open in its first winter. By November, the projectionist union was either on strike or locked out. In January 1955, a loud explosion during a movie was made by "a home-made bomb or large

I'm not sure when the Evans sign got a "New" on top of it, or even what was new. 1972 photo by Anthony L. Vazquez-Hernandez.

firecracker," according to a county sheriff. Stanger said it caused no damage except a hole in the ground.

In July 1955, two Kansas City men were jailed after they were allegedly spotted placing a sack containing 12 sticks of dynamite in a patch of weeds near the drive-in's fence. In March 1957, someone threw a stick of dynamite wrapped in tape over the gate at the snack bar, but the Evans was closed and damage was minor.

The Evans had a strange layout, as seen in this 1964 photo. © Historic-Aerials.com, used by permission.

On the other hand, an explosion May 9, 1957 ripped off a 6-foot section of corrugated fence, which narrowly missed a car leaving the drive-in. Stanger continued to insist on running his own projectors, and a union representative went on record as resenting any suggestion that his group was responsible for the blast.

That was the last I've found about labor troubles and explosions (not necessarily related) at the Evans. In 1961, Stanger completely remodeled his concession stand. In 1965, the Minicast Corp. of Wheat Ridge installed a grid of AM radio antennas to deliver sound to the viewing field.

At the end of the 1966 season, Stanger leased the Evans to Highland Theatres and moved to Estes Park, where he ran the Lake Estes Drive-In. Highland quickly signed union contracts for the Evans and picked Jan Slager to manage it. Slager had formerly managed the Centennial and had founded a business that made drive-in intermission tapes.

Before the 1977 season, De Lux Theatres, owned by Frank McLaughlin, took over the Evans and started carload pricing. The drive-in hung in there for another five years before closing, making way for the large grocery store that's still there today.

Havana Drive-In

Listed under the city of Aurora.

Lake Shore Drive-In

Listed under the city of Edgewater.

Monaco Drive-In

Opened: July 13, 1950

Closed: Oct. 4, 1977

Capacity: 750 cars

After getting turned down on a plan to build near the future Valley Drive-In, Paul Rothman, Lem Lee and Robert Otwell convinced the Denver zoning board to let them build the first drive-in within the city limits. When they started building it in the spring of 1950, they expected to call it the Kar-Vu, the same as the drive-in they opened that April in Brighton. Within a couple of months, the name changed.

When the Monaco opened at 40th Avenue and Monaco Parkway, it held about 750 cars and had seats for 150 walk-ins. Its concession stand was one of the first to offer its food cafeteria style along a 60-

Lee Theatres reused the illustration at the top of its 4th Birthday ad two months later for the grand opening of the Wadsworth in Arvada. Did the two drive-ins really look that much alike?

foot, horseshoe-shaped counter. The owners deliberately blocked off the view of the screen from the concession stand to help keep the line moving.

As with most early Denver-area drive-ins, the Monaco was a huge success. One night in 1951, its operators had to turn away 1320 cars because the lot was already full.

In October 1952, Lee filed suit against four Wolfberg-owned drive-ins and United Artists, saying he was locked out of getting UA films on a timely basis. In November, Lee built his home at the Monaco.

For its fourth birthday, celebrated a few months early in April 1954, the Monaco offered 4-cent admission with four movies and four cartoons. So many cars waited in line for early arrivals to leave that the drive-in kept showing movies till four in the morning, and snack bar income made up for any lost ticket sales.

After receiving "a fair sized amount," Lee settled his lawsuit in May 1954. The next spring, long and heavy dust storms damaged thousands of speakers over the course of a month. In January 1956, Lee and Rothman sued eight distributors and two theater companies again about getting movies on a timely basis. One month later, Wolfberg bought them out.

By 1963, there was still a lot of empty land around the Monaco. © HistoricAerials.com, used by permission.

The Monaco stayed under Wolfberg's Compass umbrella for 20 years. They installed 70mm projectors in 1961. In 1976, when Wolfberg's lease ran out, Rothman took over again and operated it for two more seasons. When the Monaco closed, its land was leased to Monaco Parking, which served Stapleton Airport about a mile away. Warehouses occupy the site today.

Motorena / North Drive-In

Listed under the city of Westminster.

North Star Drive-In

Listed under the city of Thornton.

South Drive-In

Listed under the city of Englewood.

Valley Drive-In

Opened: June 6, 1953

Closed: June 19, 1977

Capacity: 1000 cars

The Valley, named for the nearby Valley Highway (now I-25), holds a special place in my heart because it was the closest Colorado drive-in to what would become Carload.com World Headquarters, although it was long gone before I moved in.

Back then, Denver was expanding to the southeast, and drive-in developers knew they wanted to serve the new market. In 1950, the Denver zoning board rejected a drive-in plan presented by Paul Rothman and Lem Lee, who with Elden Menagh would build the Kar-Vu in Brighton later that year. Two years later, plans for the Welshire, to be built by Lake Shore owner Anthony Archer, were blocked by Arapahoe County after neighborhood opposition.

At the same time the Welshire was going nowhere, Wolfberg Theatres was more successful in adding another drive-in to its Compass chain. It built the Valley, with room for 1000 cars, east of the Valley Highway on Evans Avenue near Monaco Parkway. It was the first Denver area drive-in with a second-story projection booth and a curved screen.

The official grand opening came after a couple of weeks of making sure everything was working right.

Wolfberg quietly opened the Valley on June 6, 1953, then held an official grand opening on June 25 with free candy for the children, flowers for the ladies, and cigarettes for the men. Its audience in the early years were mostly residents of the nearby new housing developments and students from the University of Denver just a couple of miles away on Evans.

What followed was a couple of quiet decades of corporate ownership as the neighborhood around the Valley changed. Alan Flohr, who once ran the drive-in for Wolfberg, later told the *Golden Transcript*, "Back in '65, it used to be surrounded by rolling hills and was nice and dark. Now the highway goes right past and there's a supermarket next to it."

In 1966, Wolfberg hired Menagh, then managing the Sunset in Fort Collins, to manage the Valley. Ray Wagner was the manager in 1977 when Wolfberg closed the Valley, citing increased taxes and land values. The site was promptly cleared and developed into a shopping center. A small dentist's office sits where the Valley's screen used to be.

Wadsworth Indoor Drive-In

Listed under the city of Arvada.

West Drive-In

Listed under the city Lakewood.

West Colfax Drive-In

Also listed under the city of Lakewood.

Dove Creek

Dove Creek is the largest town and county seat for Dolores County, which isn't very populous. Pinto bean farming matches the local soil and climate, a fact Native Americans had figured out and World War I veterans rediscovered by the 1920s. Only about 700 people lived in town when its drive-in arrived, and only about that many live there today.

Auto-Vu Drive-In

Opened: May 22, 1953

Closed: October 1978?

Capacity: 130 cars

On the far west side of the state, this was one of the few Colorado drive-ins in the Salt Lake City film service area rather than Denver's. (The other two were in Cortez.) That was a good match for the Auto-Vu, which began and ended its life with Utah-based owners.

Elizabeth Young of tiny La Sal UT and her son Robert built a small drive-in three miles west of Dove Creek on US 160. It held just 100 cars when it opened, playing the same movie twice a night. There was a snack bar in addition to the projection room. Its screen faced north, toward the

The grand opening ad for the Auto-Vu in the *Dove Creek Press*.

highway and a narrow viewing field. The Youngs remodeled before reopening for the 1954 season, adding a new ticket office, a new fence, and more speakers.

After two seasons, Robert Young left Dove Creek in the winter of 1954-55, traveling to Holbrook AZ to build the Western Star Drive-In there. (**Crossover alert:** The full story is in my 2019 book *Drive-Ins of Route 66.*) After failing in Holbrook, he brought all of that equipment down to Buckeye AZ, where he opened another Western Star. That one survived until 1959.

Since this is the Colorado drive-in book, let's return to Dove Creek. In its 1955-56 edition, the *Theatre Catalog* listed the Auto-Vu with a 130-car capacity and under the owner- ship of Neil Bolt and George Armstrong. The 1957 *Motion Picture Almanac* showed only Neil Bolt and a capacity of 100. Bolt owned the indoor Empire in Dove Creek, so it's natural that he would have purchased the Auto-Vu from the Youngs.

Chuck Henning's "Home Town" newspaper column had a short anecdote about the Auto-Vu in August 1957. Two youngsters on horseback tried to sneak in without paying, but were ejected and ended up paying a $10 fine each. The movie was a western, of course.

The top and bottom parts of the Auto Vu's last ad in the *Dove Creek Press*. Reminds me of something from a fanzine.

In the 1962 *Almanac*, the owner name changed from Bolt to his sister, Mrs. Maxine Roush, who had run for Dove Creek mayor in 1960 but received just 29 votes. In 1963, Bolt Theatres of Dove Creek qualified for a $19,000 Small Business Administration development loan for a drive-in theater. I wonder what they did to spruce up the Auto-Vu.

In 1977, after a decade of editions without owner names, the *Almanac* listed the Auto-Vu with the unlikely capacity of 200 cars and Howe's Theatres of Monticello UT as the owner. The drive-in fell off the *Almanac* list in the 1978 edition, but it was still advertising in the *Dove Creek Press* and Monticello's *San Juan Record*. On Aug. 25, 1978, the Auto-Vu ran its last newspaper ad with listings through Oct. 14.

Durango

The town of Durango has always been about trains. It pretty much got its start when the Denver and Rio Grande Railroad chose its location for a station. In the winter and spring of 1881-82, railroad workers blasted and bridged 45 miles of track through the mountains and valleys to Silverton in eight months. The Durango & Silverton Narrow Gauge Railroad still operates a tourist train over this National Historic Landmark.

Basin / Knox / Bell Drive-In

Opened: June 23, 1950

Closed: 1962

Capacity: 350 cars

The projector booth was on the north (right) side of the single-story building in the viewing field. I love the mountains in the background of this circa 1950 photo, courtesy Animas Museum photo archives, DiFerdinando Collection.

Ted Knox of Denver got together a group including Joseph Kelly and C. M. Trosper to build the Basin Drive-In, on US 550 just south of the La Plata County Fairgrounds at Junction Creek. It had a one-story projection building with its concessions and rest rooms all on its south side. By the end of the Basin's first season, Knox bought out his partners and said that he planned to let his wife manage the drive-in in 1951.

When spring rolled around, it was Ted's son Rodney who was running the Basin. In 1954, Ted installed a flashy $6000 marquee to the drive-in, and I'll bet that's when he renamed it the Knox. Meanwhile, Rodney fell in love and married a local woman; their first son arrived in December 1955. They lived next to the screen tower, and patrons sometimes saw them out front as they bought their tickets at the box office.

Before the 1958, Ted leased the Knox to Rio Grande Enterprises, and before the year was out, it was advertising as the Bell in the Fort Lewis A&M College student newspaper. In 1960, *Boxoffice* said that John Wallace had taken over the Bell from Ted Knox. John Timms visited Denver in 1962 to book movies for the Bell, but in 1963, the drive-in disappeared from the *Durango Herald* and the phone book. Durango High School replaced the Bell, and it's still there today.

Rocket Drive-In

Opened: March 10, 1957

Closed: October 2004

Capacity: 400 cars.

Leonard Scales must have been doing well in Grand Junction, where he opened its Rocket Drive-In in April 1955. The next year, his brother Jack also came up from Texas to take a look around, and he was so impressed that he went looking to buy a drive-in of his own. That search must have been unsuccessful, because by the end of 1956, Jack had begun building his own Rocket, with help from Leonard, this time in Durango.

Durango's Rocket opened on the east side of town on US 550/160. Its screen faced north-northeast, and the Animas River flowed west and south of the viewing field. Estimates of its capacity varied from 250 to 400, but aerial

My favorite part of the Rocket was the view of the cliffs on the other side of the Animas River. 1998 photo by the author.

photos indicate that the field didn't change from 1960 until it closed. At some point in the 1980s, the screen was moved closer to the projection building.

The Scales family ran the Rocket for all of 48 seasons. Leonard's daughter Melanie took over after a while, and toward the end, Melanie's daughter Amy Raso was assistant manager.

A sale to Target fell through in 2000, but everyone knew that the Rocket's days were numbered. Even though attendance was strong, Melanie kept the Rocket on the market. It finally sold near the end of the 2004 season, with an eye to condominium development, though a "10 acres for sale" sign remained there for the next several years. The Rocket Pointe Apartments, built in 2019, occupy the site today. Fort Lewis College restored the Rocket's sign and installed it in the Rocket Grille inside of its Student Union.

Edgewater

The "water" in Edgewater is Sloan Lake, which is now across Sheridan Boulevard. According to legend, in 1861, farmer Thomas Sloan dug a gusher of a well, which flooded 200 acres. Back then the lake extended into the future Edgewater, which incorporated in 1901. One of the city's first actions was building wooden boardwalks to line its muddy streets.

Lake Shore Drive-In

Opened: July 6, 1951

Closed: Oct. 8, 1985

Capacity: 1000 cars

In 1947, Gene O'Fallon bought 36 acres near Sloan Lake at $100 per acre. Within a few years, he sold 10 of those acres at $1000 each to two men who were planning a drive-in. Anthony "Tony" Archer and Joe Decker, who owned the Civic Theaters chain, broke ground in October 1950. After a few delays in the spring, the Lake Shore opened in the first week of July.

The Lake Shore had an 80x60-foot wooden screen facing a field that could hold 1000 cars. Lights adorned each speaker post, many with in-car heaters, and a lighted walkway led patrons through the center of the field to the Terrace café in the concession building. The

Boxoffice ran a two-page spread on the opening of the Lake Shore on Nov. 24, 1951. It saluted the builders for staying within Nat'l Production Authority limits by using less than two tons of steel and 200 pounds of copper to build the drive-in.

drive-in also had a 200-seat section for pedestrians and bike-riders; it included a bike rack.

All through the following winter, the Lake Shore stayed open, thanks mainly to those in-car heaters. In January 1952, a Denver restaurant company sued over the name "Terrace." Soon the drive-in's owners renamed the café the Shore. In 1955, the Lake Shore widened its screen to 120 feet, calling it the largest west of Chicago.

In December 1956, the owners looked back on the Lake Shore's first 2000 nights, noting that thanks to those heaters, it had been thwarted by weather on only 16 of them. A month later, they sold the drive-in and its land for $450,000 to Charles "C. U." Yaeger of Atoz Theatres.

Yaeger, also president of Atlas Theatres, was best known as the inventor of Bank Night.

For the next few years, the drive-in sometimes tussled with nearby businesses over bright lights. The real problem came on May 12, 1963, when an afternoon fire destroyed the screen tower. The Lake Shore quickly rebuilt with a fireproof metal screen and reopened on June 29.

Commonwealth Theatres added the Lake Shore to its Denver-area drive-in holdings in 1980, but by then Edgewater officials were saying that they'd prefer a business that provided more tax revenue than a drive-in. Its land was listed for sale for years, and someone must have finally bought it after the 1985 season. A King Soopers grocery store occupies the site today.

Englewood

As mentioned earlier in the book, Englewood was the first Colorado base for the Alexander Film Company and biplane manufacturer Alexander Industries. Before that, it was the home to a gravity-powered streetcar. A horse would pull the car up a mile-long steep hill on Broadway, then get loaded on a platform at the back of the car before it coasted back downhill.

South Drive-In

Opened: July 1, 1949

Closed: Sept. 30, 1984

Capacity: 850 cars

Wolfberg Theatres had opened the East in 1947, and the West in 1948. It bought and renamed the North in late

What was left of the South marquee watched over a green-house until it was razed with the rest of the drive-in. Photo by Kenneth James Mitchell.

1948. Since Wolfberg was going to name this chain the Compass Drive-Ins, only one direction was left.

The Arapahoe County Fair Association owned the land that Wolfberg chose for building the South. The 1000-car drive-in sat across Belleview from the county fairgrounds in the southwest corner of Englewood. For years, the South paid the Fair 3½ cents for every $1 of ticket sales and 25 cents of every dollar spent at the concession stand.

When it opened, the South had a pony ring in addition to the standard children's playground. To help promote the drive-in late in its first season, its manager hired airplanes to drop free passes after school to see a program of Disney films. The *Denver Post* reported in 1955 that, against a backdrop of a labor dispute, an explosion blew up the South's ticket booth after it had closed for the night. That dispute appears to be have been worked out that year. In 1962, Wolfberg added in-car heaters to keep the South running all winter long.

The South spent its life in otherwise quiet corporate ownership. Commonwealth took over Wolfberg's Compass drive-ins in 1979, and the drive-in closed after the 1984 season. Athletic fields occupy the site today.

Estes Park

The gateway to Rocky Mountain National Park, Estes Park is a nice place to visit all by itself. The aerial tramway that takes customers partway up Prospect Mountain has the right balance of natural beauty and touristy kitsch for my tastes. And for full-on retro thrills, the giant rainbow slide at Fun City provides the same rush it did 35+ years ago.

Lake Estes Drive-In

Opened: May 15, 1953

Closed: 1990

Capacity: 302 cars

D. D. "Ted" Shanks came to Estes Park in 1951 looking to buy the Ford dealership there. When that didn't work, he bought a piece of land just east of town in 1952 and built the Lake Estes with Lewis Teuscher. At the time, it had one of the highest elevations (~7500 feet) of any drive-in.

Teuscher and Shanks gave away flown-in Hawaiian orchids to all ladies attending the Grand Opening of the Lake Estes. All subsequent stories about the drive-in mention only Mr. and Mrs. Shanks as the owners. One night in 1955, Shanks gave free admission to anyone with a hearing aid. In June, he donated the night's profits (as opposed to revenue) to the local Chamber of Commerce building fund. In September that year, an unattended car from Peoria IL rolled into the projection booth, causing damage to the cinder-block building and equipment though no one was hurt.

I really liked the logo that the Lake Estes used in its *Estes Park Trail* ads.

Every summer, Shanks would come to town to run the drive-in, and every off-season, he went somewhere else, sometimes his original home in Iowa, sometimes to Palm Springs CA. He also finally got that Estes Park Ford dealership. Dreams can come true.

Perhaps Shanks's interest in the drive-in faded after he got busy with other local businesses. Lee Lindecrantz leased the Lake Estes in 1960, then the drive-in stopped advertising in the *Estes Park Trail* in 1961. The drive-in's restaurant, also called the Lake Estes, continued to operate at the front of the property.

R. L. "Mickey" Stanger, who had built and operated the Evans in Denver, bought the Lake Estes in early 1964. The obituary for his wife Ola said that the new purchase "became Mickey's 'hobby' that barely paid the taxes." After the 1966 season, "they leased the Evans … so they could both be in Estes Park."

In 1968, the Stangers bought the local, historic indoor Park Theatre. Just before the 1969 season, high winds knocked down the Lake Estes screen, but Stanger rebuilt. The drive-in kept on rolling for another couple of decades before closing for good. Their family still runs the Park.

Intermission:
"Almost" Drive-Ins

Every drive-in included in this book actually opened for business. But there were at least a dozen others, reported to be in the final planning or construction phase, that never showed a single movie.

There's a chance I might be wrong about one or two of these. If you know one that opened, please let me know. Otherwise, just enjoy this list of wishful thinking:

1948

Elden Menagh, who owned the indoor Star in Fort Lupton, announced in April that he would build a $75,000 drive-in in Greeley. A month later, he decided against it, buying a Fort Lupton chicken ranch instead.

John Wolfberg announced in May that he was building a drive-in north of Denver on Federal Avenue. The Motorena somehow beat him to the punch; before the year was out, he bought it and renamed it the North.

In lieu of drive-ins that never existed, here's a 1950s photo of a chicken ranch. Maybe Elden Menagh's looked like this. Photo courtesy Orange County Archives.

1949

Boxoffice wrote that "local business men" Floyd Davis and Nat Jones broke ground on a 400-car drive-in "three blocks east of Highway 85, just north of Eagle Tail airport" in Springfield CO. That turned out to be the 85 Drive-In in Raton NM, which is very different.

1950

Boxoffice said in January that "J. C. Parker and E. F. Hardwick" were building a new drive-in in Fort Morgan. I've got no idea who they were. By March, the magazine said that John Roberts, who owned indoor theaters in Brush and Fort Morgan, would have a 400-car drive-in ready for spring. That got delayed, Jake Bauer beat Roberts to open a drive-in there, and Roberts bought Bauer's two years later.

In August, Lionel Semon, who had built Pueblo's first two drive-ins, got a building permit from Pueblo County for a third one just west of town on Highway 96. He didn't follow through on that one.

1951

The Korean War, and the National Production Authority in particular, severely curtailed new construction, even the imaginary kind.

1952

Anthony Archer, co-owner of the Lake Shore and vice-president of Atoz Amusements, proposed the Welshire, a new $300,000 drive-in just west of the Valley Highway on a 14-acre site. Neighborhood opposition to the project killed it, or at least delayed it until Wolfberg's Valley opened in June 1953 a few blocks down the street.

1953

The Maizeland Drive-In was set to begin construction in May a mile north of US 24 in Colorado Springs. Again, neighbors' protests to the county zoning commissioners blocked the deal.

Here's another drive-in feature that I'm not sure ever appeared in Colorado — open-air concession stands. And did any of them have such a crowd of sophisticated, debonair adults? Older drive-in intermission reels sometimes included images such as the one above, and new drive-ins of the 1950s often boasted of their indoor refreshment centers as though that was an innovation. So, maybe?

On the other hand, in July, Peter Nachtrab won county zoning approval for a two-screen drive-in on North Nevada Avenue, also in Colorado Springs. After that didn't happen, Nachtrab moved to Toledo OH in 1956.

1954

Joe Giordano, who owned the indoor Main Theatre in Walsenberg, was reported by three trade magazines in August to be building a 250-car drive-in west of town, with opening day tentatively set for September. That sounds a lot like the Trail, which Frank Piazza built in the summer of 1963.

1955

In January, Harold Olson and Kenneth Swartz from Nebraska were building a 400-car drive-in in Florence. Today, nobody in Florence knows anything about this project, reported by two magazines.

1956

Bob Walker, who owned the indoor Uintah Theatre in Fruita, announced plans in February to build a 250-car drive-in on land he owned three miles east of town "between Rhone School and the highway," *Boxoffice* wrote. Was that was related to the Monument, which opened between Grand Junction and Fruita in 1958?

1957

Boxoffice said that Phil Belt, owner of the Mancos Theatre, "is completing a 250-car drive-in theatre." If that name sounds familiar, Belt was the former teenage owner of the Independent in Cortez. Today, no one in Mancos can find anything about Belt's second drive-in.

1965

The Jefferson County Board of County Commissioners approved commercial zoning in March for a 1000-car drive-in to be built in southwest Denver by Bear Valley Drive-In Theater, a Wolfberg subsidiary, near Dartmouth Avenue and South Sheridan Boulevard. In June, a district court judge overturned the rezoning on a technicality, to the delight of opposing neighborhood groups.

Also in March, Fox Intermountain Theaters planned to build a drive-in in Golden in the area "between Routes 6 and 40," according to Golden's *Colorado Transcript*.

1973

In a March list of theaters under construction, *Boxoffice* wrote, "Meeker – 300-seat indoor, plus drive-in, Ron Gitchell." Gitchell lost the election for mayor of Meeker in 1974.

Fort Collins

The US Army's Camp Collins, named for the officer in charge of Fort Laramie, began protecting the Overland Trail around 1862. After a flood destroyed the camp in June 1864, it moved downriver to the future city's site. Fort Collins, the fort, never had any walls, and it was decommissioned in 1867. Fort Collins the city grew to be the fourth-largest in the state, and is today the home of Colorado State University and over 20 craft breweries.

Sunset Drive-In

Opened: Oct. 5, 1948

Closed: 1979?

Capacity: 500 cars

Joe LaConte brought in a couple of drive-in builders from Utah to form the Collins Drive-In Theatre Corporation, which built the Sunset southeast of Fort Collins. The drive-in included a modest 50x38-foot screen erected on the hill facing Stuart Street. LaConte managed the Sunset and lived in a house adjacent to it.

At the end of 1950, LaConte sued the corporation for over $55,000 on promissory notes and salary claims. The corporation dissolved the next year after transferring ownership of the Sunset to LaConte. The next decade passed fairly quietly, with only the usual dose of vandalism and missing speakers.

Just before the 1960 season, Claude Graves and Wilbur Williams, who owned Boulder's Holiday and Motorena drive-ins, bought the Sunset, though LaConte retained its land.

Detail of the Sunset grand opening ad, which also said there were then over 500 US drive-ins, up from just 20 two years earlier.

The Fort Collins *Coloradoan* story about the sale said that the newcomers refinished the screen, touched up the painting on the grounds, and added speakers. "There are 500 speaker poles, but … only enough speakers for 300 cars were in operation" under the former owner.

That story added that LaConte was moving to Denver "to pursue various business interests." One of those was a Westminster strip mall on Federal Blvd. north of 72nd Avenue. Today it's still known as the LaConte Shopping Center.

Meanwhile Graves and Williams brought in an experienced drive-in manager, Elden Menagh, who had owned the Kar-Vu in Brighton for its first five years. Menagh also managed the Sunset for five years before leaving to manage Denver's Valley in 1966.

1966 was also the year that the recently formed Highland Theatres purchased the Sunset along with its sister drive-ins in Boulder. Highland would eventually own 10 of Colorado's drive-ins before selling out to Kansas City-based Commonwealth Theatres in 1978. The Sunset continued only a little while longer; by 1980, it was gone.

Starlite / Holiday Twin Drive-In

Opened: April 10, 1968

~~Closed:~~ active!

Capacity: 800 cars

Colorado State's Hughes Stadium, on the far west side of town, was under construction when the Starlite opened across Overland Trail. Former Fort Collins resident Paul Cory had returned to build the single-screen drive-in.

High winds blew off part of the screen tower in the spring of 1969. I don't know whether it was a coincidence that Highland Theatres took over operations in April that year.

The Holiday Twin sign looks about the same today as it did in this 1997 photo by the author.

By the mid-1970s, Cory was ready to sell. One deal in late 1975 fell through because a bank declined a loan. Highland added a second screen and split the viewing field in 1976, now calling the drive-in the Holiday Twin, the same name as one of Highland's drive-ins in Boulder. In 1978, Cory continued to advertise the drive-in for sale.

Enter Wesley Webb. Drive-in theater owners often flew airplanes as a way to save the cost of shipping heavy reels of film, but Webb was an experienced pilot before he got into the theater business. He bought and sold planes, and he saw drive-ins as investment opportunities – "big pieces of ground that make money" while they appreciate in value.

Somebody told Webb about Cory's desire to sell the Holiday Twin, so he flew to Fort Collins to check it out. The story Webb told was that when they were negotiating, Cory said, "What I really want is just your airplane." They made the trade, and Webb owned another drive-in.

Years later, Webb said that he added the Holiday Twin as a tax write-off and a place for his son to learn the movie business. But he fell in love in Fort Collins, getting married there in 1997. When Webb sold the rest of his drive-ins in 2001, he kept the Holiday Twin, promising that he'd never sell it. He still owned it when he passed away in 2019, and his widow still owns it today.

Fort Morgan

Camp Tyler started as a military post along the Overland stagecoach route in 1865. It was soon renamed Camp Wardwell. In 1866 it became Fort Morgan, named for a colonel who was killed by a gas leak in a St. Louis hotel. The fort closed in 1868, and its sod walls slowly disintegrated. When the railroad arrived in 1880, the town of Fort Morgan sprang up around the old fort site.

Bauer's / Valley Drive-In

Opened: May 18, 1950

Closed: Oct. 28, 2010

Capacity: 350 cars

In early 1950, in Fort Morgan, the race was on to build the town's first drive-in. On one side was John Roberts, owner of indoor theaters in town and in nearby Brush. The day after Roberts started construction, local grocer Jacob "Jake" Bauer started work on another drive-in practically next door.

Improbably, the grocer beat the theater man. Bauer's Drive-In opened to the public a day ahead of schedule. The next day, at the Grand Opening, a twister hit, causing a short pause while Bauer rebuilt. Meanwhile, Roberts' project had been delayed, and later that year, it was effectively blocked by the National Production

Except for a different paint color on the sign, the Valley also looks about the same today as it did in this 1997 photo by the author, but unlike the Holiday Twin, the Valley is closed.

Authority, formed to
allocate scarce materials
during the Korean War.

The logo that Bauer's used
at the top of its ads in the
Brush News-Tribune.

That fall, Bauer toured
drive-ins in California,
Arizona, and New Mexico
to check out their in-car
heaters. He must have been
impressed, because he
announced in December
that Bauer's had installed heaters and would stay open
all winter.

In 1951, Bauer was busy building the Brush Drive-In
in Brush. In November that year, Bauer's Drive-In
sponsored a talent show on a large stage erected in front
of the screen. But in January 1952, Morgan bought out
both of Jake Bauer's drive-ins. The story in the *Brush
News-Tribune* said that "Bauer said operation of the two
theaters was too much work for him and he would now
devote his time to Bauer's Market."

Now Roberts owned all five theaters in Morgan
County, and he shut down Bauer's to remodel it. He
reopened the drive-in as the Valley and installed his sons
Gene and John Jr. as co-managers.

In 1959, Herbert Boehm bought the Valley from
Roberts and installed his son Milton as the owner /
manager, a job he kept for 40 years. Milt was a character.
In the summer of 1977, someone threw beer bottles at the
Valley sign and stole some of its letters. Boehm took out a
Fort Morgan Times ad saying he'd offer a $500 reward for
the letter thieves, or they could return them that
weekend, "no questions asked." That Monday morning,
he found the letters in a sack at the drive-in.

In 1999, Boehm sold the Valley, along with the
indoor Cover, to locals Mike and Mak Tibbetts. The new

owners put a fresh coat of paint on the sign, and redesigned the concession stand with a throwback 50s vibe. A windstorm destroyed the screen in early 2001, and they scrambled to rebuild it two days before the scheduled season opener.

I guess Mike and Mak Tibbetts didn't like the Valley sign's previous shade of green. It still has that hole in the corner, same as Delta's Tru Vu. 2005 photo by jeterga.

In the spring of 2011, Mike Tibbetts announced that the Valley would not reopen, citing the cost of operating it and the impending switch to digital projection. Today, the Valley sits intact, waiting to see if it will be reopened or razed.

Fountain

The town of Fountain, at the confluence of Jimmy Camp Creek and Fountain Creek, was founded in 1859, the same year as Denver and Colorado City. It was almost wiped off the map on May 14, 1888 when the fire from a train collision ignited a car loaded with explosives. Residents in Monument, 33 miles away, reported being awakened by the blast. Fountain rebuilt and incorporated in 1903.

Vista Vue / Vista View Drive-In

Opened: June 29, 1956

Closed: Oct. 31, 1984

Capacity: 650 cars

Colorado Springs already had five active drive-ins when William Claiborne started building his own a few miles south, across the highway from the community of Security in present-day Fountain. It featured a curved 120x68-foot screen, immodestly

The top of the Vista Vue's grand opening ad.

described as "the largest CinemaScope screen of its kind in the West." A miniature train circled the drive-in on a long dirt ridge with a tunnel under the tower.

At some point, I'm going to have to mention its name, so I'll get it over with here. Trade publications reported that Claiborne would call his drive-in the Vista View. But in late June, its huge Grand Opening ads in the *Colorado Springs Gazette-Telegraph* called it the Vista Vue. Through the following decades, it sometimes advertised as the Vista View, other times reverting to Vista Vue. Once, on a page with two ads, it used both spellings! If I ever found a photo of its sign, I'd go with whatever it said. In its absence, I'll stick with Vista Vue.

Westland Theatres quickly gobbled up the Vista Vue to add to its other Colorado Springs-area theaters, and then the drive-in settled in to a quiet, corporate-owned life. In October 1984, its land was rezoned as a business park; its final program was *The Texas Chainsaw Massacre* and *The Evil Dead*. In 1990, the *Gazette* wrote that the site was still dormant and "the speaker standards have literally been put out to pasture, piled high like junked cars." Nothing remains of the Vista Vue today.

Glenwood Springs

Glenwood Springs was named after the founder's wife's home town of Glenwood IA. It's got a nice Amtrak station, Glenwood Caverns Adventure Park, and museums, but what most folks picture when they think of this town is the Glenwood Hot Springs Resort pool, the world's largest hot springs pool.

Canyon Drive-In

Opened: Sept. 12, 1950

Closed: Sept. 10, 1979

Capacity: 400 cars

Gibralter Theatres, a confederation of mid-sized theater owners, owned the indoor Glen Theater, managed by Don Cornwall. In 1950, when seemingly everyone was building drive-ins, Cornwall saw the Canyon built for Glenwood Springs. It was at the west edge of town on Highway 6/24. The north-facing screen was a modest 50-feet with a playground in front. "Moon-Glo" lights provided enough

The Canyon in 1960.
© Historicaerials.com, used by permission.

background light for patrons to get from their cars to the concession stand and back.

And that's about it. The Canyon led a quiet life with one corporate owner and one manager. Its seasons were relatively short, and on the Monday after Labor Day 1979, the drive-in closed and didn't reopen. The Glenwood Springs Mall occupies the site today.

Grand Junction

For a few weeks during the summers of 1958 and 1959, there were twice as many active drive-ins in Grand Junction as there were indoor theaters. But the Mesa and Cooper (now the Avalon) survive to this day, while all four drive-ins are long gone. Heck, the Monument barely made it 15 months.

Chief Drive-In

Opened: March 21, 1952

Closed: Sept. 4, 1989

Capacity: 450 cars

Westland Theatres first announced that they were going to build a drive-in on this site, on US 6-24 (North Avenue) four blocks east of the Starlite, in April 1950. That was while Westland's first drive-in, the 8th Street in Colorado Springs, was still under construction. Their Grand Junction project was delayed for some reason, probably because the National Production Authority temporarily blocked a lot of building projects during the Korean War.

When the Chief finally opened in March 1952, it had a curved screen. Its concession stand sold all of the usual drive-in goodies, plus "a special plate lunch." The Chief's neon sign up front showed an Indian chief's head with the movie signboard below. A grassy median behind the sign separated the entrance and exit lanes. Lighted domes indicated the ramp numbers. The playground sat in front of the screen; in later years, it moved behind the concession stand, then left the lot.

A heavy card poster from the Chief's 1952 opening. Photo by Nick Genova.

The Chief spent its corporate-owned years fairly quietly, with only the usual break-ins and hold-ups to generate newspaper stories. In early 1985, Commonwealth Theatres bought Westland's theatres, and a year later, Cannon / United Artists bought the Commonwealth circuit. Without advance notice, the Chief closed after the 1989 season and simply didn't reopen. Medical offices occupy the site today.

Monument Drive-In

Opened: June 15, 1957

Closed: Sept. 15, 1958

Capacity: 350 cars

Records of the Monument are a little spotty, which seems appropriate. The last drive-in to open in Grand Junction was also the first to close, and some accounts suggested that it wasn't the most attractive entertainment choice.

Guy Carlucci Jr. of Fruita, the son of an immigrant turkey farmer, partnered with A. B. Moore of Colorado

Springs to build the Monument at a cost of about $45,000. They built it about a half mile west of the city limits on Highway 6/50. The screen, which pointed southwest, was 97x57 feet, accommodating CinemaScope films. The viewing field was bound by 21½ Road to the east and Pritchard Wash to the northwest.

Guy Sr. passed away three days after the Monument opened. After an outwardly uneventful season, the drive-in closed in October.

The Monument was slow to reopen in 1958, finally advertising on June 5 that it was under new management. There was another hiatus from July 30 until August 9, when its ad said, "Now open / Improved light and projection". Again, the season passed without other notice, and the drive-in closed in September, never to reopen.

A 1976 recap of drive-ins in Grand Junction's *Daily Sentinel* said of the Monument, "This theater did not do well, perhaps because of its location". It's just as likely that Grand Junction couldn't support four drive-ins, and the other three already had regular customers.

Guy Jr. later became a Fruita historian, but his obituary in 2008 made no mention of the drive-in he co-created. I haven't found any other traces of A. B. Moore. All I have is a name, which is more than I know about the 1958 new management. Today, the Monument site is an empty lot, and the graveled entrance is all that remains of the drive-in.

The short-lived Monument as it looked in 1958. © Historicaerials.com, used by permission.

Rocket Drive-In

Opened: April 16, 1955

Closed: Sept. 7, 1987

Capacity: 350 cars

Leonard Scales came up from Lubbock TX in the winter of 1955 to join Grand Junction's drive-in boom. He built it practically next door to the Chief. When it opened, the Rocket had a wide, curved 80x40-foot screen, while Scales called the largest in western Colorado. Its narrow viewing field held 350 cars with room to expand to 500.

Except for that time a guy confessed to the Rocket's security guy that he had killed his mother-in-law (at her home), the drive-in's first couple of decades were fairly quiet. In February 1976, Scales leased the Rocket to Westland Theatres, which owned the Chief across the highway. In 1985, Commonwealth bought Westland's theaters, so it owned the Rocket for a year.

Westland/Commonwealth's 10-year lease had expired by February 1986, so Leonard Scales allowed his daughter and son-in-law, Melanie and Alan Gates, to

The Rocket's grand opening ad in the Grand Junction *Daily Sentinel.*

manage the Rocket for what became its final two seasons. The following spring, Walmart announced that it would build its first Grand Junction store on the Rocket site. Later reports said that Scales received $1 million for his drive-in's land. That Walmart is still there.

Starlite Drive-In

Opened: Aug. 2, 1947

Moved: May 5, 1959

Closed: Oct. 18, 1966

Capacity: 450 cars

Clarence and Loyd Files never saw a drive-in movie before they built their own drive-in theater. In 1947, hearing about the postwar craze reaching the West, the brothers drove over to the ozoner that was closest to completion, the Autorium in Salt Lake City, to get ideas. And then they built one almost from scratch on the east side of town next to the new Veterans Hospital.

Clarence and Loyd scrounged around for materials to build a 40x30-foot screen, covered it with plywood, painted it white, and hired a crane to hoist it into place. They built their own ramps and a little projection building with restrooms. For speaker poles, they cut off flue pipes, ran wires through the center, and embedded them in concrete bases. Ted Knox, a man who would have a hand in many

OPENING SATURDAY 8:00 P.M.

STARLITE – Drive In
THEATRE

· First Pictures "Bedside Manner" and "Dark Alibi"

Here is the latest in theatre amusement. Room for 300 cars. Enjoy your own car, private speakers. Two shows nightly. Bring the whole family... all the kids.

Admission Prices: Adults...50¢   Children 6 to 12...11¢
Colorado's Number Two Drive-In Theatre

North Avenue   One Block East New Vets Hospital

The Starlite's modest grand opening ad in the July 31, 1947 issue of the *Daily Sentinel*.

Colorado drive-ins, supplied the five-inch in-car speakers.

The Starlite was an immediate, overwhelming hit; locals marveled that they could watch movies outside a theater building. "No one had ever seen an outdoor theatre," Loyd later recalled. "People didn't believe there could be such a thing."

The Starlite had the Grand Junction drive-in market to itself for the next four seasons. The brothers upgraded the screen to

By 1958, when this photo was taken, development had surrounded the Starlite. © Historicaerials.com, used by permission.

corrugated iron and added two more ramps, growing the drive-in's capacity from 300 cars to 450. As the 1950s went by, the Chief and the Rocket arrived, and the city expanded around the formerly remote Starlite site. And then things got weird.

In February 1959, the brothers sold the Starlite's land, and William Moore bought the screen and equipment. Moore, who had built the Uranium Drive-In in Naturita five years earlier, effectively moved the Starlite, rebuilding it on the west side of Grand Junction at 23 & G roads, reopening in time for most of the 1959 season.

Moore had brought along 300 new in-car heaters, but I don't know whether he had much chance to use them. In April 1960, after a sheriff's sale, Clarence Files took back the relocated Starlite, and he acquired the Uranium as well. Clarence moved to Naturita for a while as he ran the Uranium, sometimes leaving his wife in charge of the Starlite. (In 1966, he ran for mayor of Naturita, but finished second in the election.)

The Starlite seemed to struggle on the west side. In the summer of 1961, Gladys and Ernest Barnes bought the drive-in from Clarence, but he got it back again at the end of the 1962 season. (Though it was never explicitly stated, I presume the Files family would self-finance these sales, using the drive-in as collateral.) In 1965, A. M. Crews took over operating the Starlite for a season, but announced in early 1966 that it would not reopen. Harold Haws reversed that announcement, stepping in to manage the Starlite's final season, which ended with a Tuesday night Spanish-language double-feature. In 1967, it stayed closed.

The USGS took this photo in July 1973. The second Starlite site had already lost its screen, and its ramps had faded.

The Starlite's old west-side site remains a mostly vacant lot today. Loyd Files passed away in 2006 at the age of 107, and his name is on the Museum of the West's research library. His *Denver Post* obituary called him "one of the Western Slope's most successful businessmen."

Greeley

This town began in 1869 as the experimental Union Colony, founded by newspaper reporter Nathan Meeker. It was later renamed after Horace Greeley, Meeker's editor at the *New York Tribune*. Since 1889, Greeley has been a college town. That constant influx of new, young patrons may be part of the reason that two competing drive-ins stayed active for decades in a town of just around 20,000 people when they opened.

Greeley Drive-In

Opened: Aug. 14, 1948

Closed: 1982?

Capacity: 600 cars

In 1948, Emmett Savard and his son-in-law, Rudolph Meyer, raced theater veteran Irving Gilman to be the first to open a drive-in in Greeley. They won that race by a week, though both opened in August that year. Their Greeley Drive-In, northwest of town on then-US 34, held 400 cars with room for expansion and started with a 60x40-foot screen facing north, away from the highway.

After a short season, Savard and Meyer made some changes for 1949. New wings on either side of the screen blocked light from the road. They also improved the rest rooms, box office, and snack bar.

On June 16, 1956, a windstorm knocked down the Greeley's screen during a movie. Cars in the front rows noticed the screen starting to lean and were able to back out of the way. Manager Jack Redus said that no one was hurt, and that it was as good a time as any to replace the screen with a curved, 100-foot-wide model. That was in operation by July.

In September 1962, city officials confiscated the print of *The Immoral Mr. Teas*, which showed the backs of unclothed

In 1969, over 20 years after it opened, the Greeley was still in the middle of open fields, across the street from a golf course. © Historic-aerials.com, used by permission.

women, then playing at the Greeley. The manager at the time was Vern Hudson.

In 1974, Savard was advertising the Greeley's land for sale. Before the 1976 season, Al Provost, owner of the Kar-Vu in Brighton, took over operation of the Greeley and Greeley's indoor Hillside. The drive-in continued advertising in the *Greeley Tribune* through at least the 1981 season, then the screen came down in 1982. A Walmart sits on the old Greeley's field today.

Motorena Drive-In

Opened: Aug. 21, 1948

Closed: 1979

Capacity: 500 cars

Irving Gilman was busy in the summer of 1948. He had built the Motorena Drive-In in Westminster, he'd soon finish the Motorena Drive-In in Boulder, and in between he opened the Motorena in Greeley. When it opened, it was alone on the south side of town, across state highway 22 from Evans Cemetery. Greeley's Motorena started with a 75x65-foot screen, a playground, and a wide projection / concession stand close to the screen.

By the end of 1948, there was a flurry of activity behind the scenes. Gilman sold this Motorena to Cinema Amusements within weeks of opening. In December, several companies involved in its construction filed suit to collect over $18,000, asking that the drive-in should be sold to satisfy the debt. By May 1952, Lee Theaters, run by Lem Lee, owned this Motorena.

There were fun times at the Motorena. In September 1950, intermissions featured The "Miracle" Horse, which would seesaw on a 12-inch wide teeter totter eight feet high without letting the ends touch the ground. On Aug. 30, 1955, Ralph Patten and Wanda Miller were married on top of the concession stand at the Motorena, where they met and both worked. The movies playing that evening were: *Let's Make it Legal* and *Love That Brute*. (The Pattens celebrated their golden anniversary in 2005.)

The trademark spotted letters of the Motorena chain were part of its grand opening ad.

In an August 1956 ad in the *Windsor Beacon*, the manager wrote, "The Motorena Drive-In Theater features the only modern playground in Colorado. It contains a merry-go-round, Ferris wheel, 7 sets of swings for all ages, two large size miracle whirls, two smaller size miracle whirls, a safety climber, 3 sets of springer-type Texas broncs and 3 elephant slides."

In the spring of 1958, Lee moved his trailer to the Motorena to live there for a few summers. After the 1960 season, he moved to a home he bought in Denver.

In January 1965, Wesco Theatres, run by Carlin Smith, bought the Motorena from Lee. Cooper Highland soon absorbed Wesco, and in 1978, Commonwealth bought Cooper Highland's theaters. The Motorena's final ads in the *Greeley Tribune* were in the 1979 season. A block of 29th Street Road east of 11th Avenue runs through the middle of old Motorena site; a lot south of that road remains vacant.

Greenwood Village

Greenwood Village, named for the pioneering Greenwood Ranch nearby, incorporated in 1950 to defend itself against Denver's slow sprawl. It's the home of Fiddlers Green Amphitheatre, owned by the non-profit Museum of Outdoor Arts. Bands from Aerosmith to ZZ Top have performed there from 1988 through whenever post-Covid concerts return.

Arapahoe Drive-In

Opened: April 12, 1972

Closed: Oct. 10, 1976

Capacity: 1100 cars

The Arapahoe, built on Arapahoe Road just east of I-25, was the last addition to the Wolfberg Theatres' Compass chain, and it also had the shortest life, so I'm afraid there's not much to talk about. When Wolfberg bought its land, in the middle of empty fields back then, it sold for about $1.50 per square foot. Within a decade, it would be worth at least four times that amount.

Leonard Albertini, who ran the Denver area's first drive-in, was ready to run the Arapahoe when its construction was announced in *Boxoffice* in September 1966. After years of delays, the drive-in finally opened in April 1972 with Reed speakers on theft-proof cables and over 400 in-car heaters to operate all year.

Just five years later, Albertini declined to renew Wolfberg's lease, saying that he planned to use the land for other purposes. A hodgepodge of buildings, mostly retail and restaurants, occupy the site today.

Gunnison

Captain John Gunnison sure got a lot of things named after him. The Gunnison River flows through Gunnison Valley and goes past Gunnison, the seat of Gunnison County. The guy only spent about three days there in 1853 while looking for a railroad route through the Rocky Mountains, and the Utes killed him just a few months later. Anyway, today Gunnison is a gorgeous college town and gateway to the Crested Butte ski area.

Island Acres Drive-In

Opened: July 22, 1955

Closed: 1975?

Capacity: 320 cars

Decades after it closed, the Island Acres screen continued to face a grassy field, as in this 2009 photo by David Primus. It's gone today, but the concession building still stands.

Elmo Bevington build the Island Acres Resort, a mile west of Gunnison on US 50, in 1954. He built it partly to demonstrate the products of a US Steel subsidiary, Gunnison Homes. (That was a New Albany IN prefab home builder, founded in 1935 by Foster Gunnison, not named after the old Army captain. But I digress.)

The following year, Bevington decided to add a drive-in to the resort. His partner, Edwin Koehler, opened the Island Acres Drive-In behind the resort in July, and the opening night was a sellout. Later that year, a busload of Western State College fraternity members and their dates got in to see a movie at a carload price, which worked out to five cents per person.

In 1961, Atlas Theatres took over the operation of the drive-in. In 1964, Atlas appointed a fresh WSC graduate, Fred Gerardi, in charge of the Island Acres and the indoor West.

In May 1967, the WSC student newspaper wrote that the day after "W" Day (when students annually white-washed a rock field forming a W overlooking the college) was traditionally set aside for the opening of the drive-in. Ironically, the show that year may have been the last for a while; the Island Acres didn't advertise the next spring.

In May 1973, *Boxoffice* reported that Leonard Steele, who ran the indoor Flicka Twin in Gunnison, had purchased the Island Acres and would reopen it. The headline above the *Gunnison News-Champion* article on the announcement said that the drive-in had been closed for seven years, an obvious exaggeration. Except for another March 1975 note in *Boxoffice* referencing Steele as the owner of the Island Acres, it's hard to tell exactly when the drive-in closed because it didn't advertise in the *News-Champion*. Its concession stand still sits in a grassy field, and its old sign has been repurposed for the mobile home park next door.

Intermission: Reed Speaker Company

Colorado had an important, though overlooked role in the drive-in theater industry. It hosted two of the largest companies that repaired drive-in speakers.

The first of those businesses was started by Samuel M. Reed. He was born in 1900 in Indiana, and he worked for RCA in Colorado by the early 1930s. Back then, Reed installed Photophone equipment, RCA's standard for syncing audio with film. By 1936, he managed Photophone sales and service for the entire Denver theater territory.

During World War II, RCA gave Reed a leave of absence to run movies for the American Red Cross with former theater man Homer Ellison. In 1945, they formed the Ellison-Reed Visual Aid Service in Denver, with Ellison handling the sales and Reed the service. That didn't last long. By 1948, Reed had joined Western Service & Supply Co., an RCA equipment dealer.

I get the feeling that Reed, in his late 40s, was looking for more fulfilling work. He took a leave of

A Reed Speaker Company ad as it appeared in *Boxoffice*.

absence from Western to run the Placer Theater in
Fairplay for about a year. After he returned to Western,
he started tinkering with drive-in speakers in his garage
in Golden. Finally, in early 1953, Reed launched the
business that would become Reed's Drive-In Speaker
Service. Theater owners would ship speakers for
rebuilding and reconing (swapping in fresh speaker
cones) and get them back for much less than it would
cost to buy new speakers.

Looking at the insides of so many kinds of drive-in
speakers led Reed to invent improvements. The business
morphed into the Reed Speaker Manufacturing
Company, still with facilities in Golden. Reed patented a
new, smaller type of speaker, simplified for easier
maintenance. He registered drive-in audio patents well
into the 1970s.

Even at the peak of drive-ins, speaker repair was a
niche business, but Reed's company was not alone.
Denver man Frank Horn said he had the largest speaker
repair company in the country, if not the world. National
Speaker Reconing & Mfg. Co. reconed thousands of
drive-in speakers each year, plus speakers from other
industries. Horn had been in the electronic business since
1946, fixing radios and TV sets for ten years before
switching to drive-in speaker reconing around 1957. The
company moved from 17th Street to 15th Street in 1969
and continued to advertise in *Boxoffice* through 1970.

In 1973, Reed Speaker moved from Golden to a plant
in Lakewood. At a trade show in 1979, he demonstrated a
device that provided the benefits of FM radio sound
before most cars had FM radios; it attached to a drive-in
speaker and relayed full-fidelity audio from a transmitter
in the projection booth.

The Reed Speaker Company continued to advertise
in *Boxoffice* until Reed's death in 1995.

Hotchkiss

Soon after the Federal Government evicted the Utes from their reservation, Enos Hotchkiss and his friends swooped in to homestead the area in 1880. Enos died in January 1900, just a few months before the Town of Hotchkiss was incorporated.

Valley Drive-In

Opened: Aug. 19, 1955

Closed: 1980?

Capacity: 320 cars

Quincy Lamar and F. M. Peterson built the Valley in the summer of 1955, planning a 324-car drive-in with room to expand. Its wide screen was 80x58 feet, and its concession / projection building included the box office.

Peterson and Lamar opened the Valley to an overflow crowd, but they soon moved on to other interests. Stanley Dixon operated the Valley in 1958. The following year, Don Poulos, owner of the Paonia, was also booking movies for the Valley and Hotchkiss's indoor Princess Theatre. Poulos effectively retired in 1964 and passed away in early 1966.

And that's about all I know. A 1979 USGS topo map still included the outline of the Valley, but its screen was gone from a 1985 map.

Hudson

Hudson used to be tiny, holding maybe 500 residents when its drive-in was built, though it's up over 2500 today. Its location on a main highway and railroad line attracted plenty of businesses. One of its oldest is The Pepper Pod, built in 1913 by the Peppers family. Its second location on US 6 sold gas along with "fine food and bar service." For many years, the Pod served buffalo, harvested from the herd grazing in its back yard.

Corral Drive-In

Opened: April 25, 1952

Closed: 1961

Capacity: 250

Moldt H. Philipsen (invariably written as M. H.) started his first career as a mortician in Lincoln NE before moving to Florence CO in 1930 to own his own mortuary. After World War II, at the age of 49, he began his second career as a theater manager in Denver for Atlas Theatres at the indoor Santa Fe. When Atlas built the Kar-Vu Drive-In in Brighton, it tapped Philipsen to manage it.

Philipsen ran the Kar-Vu for two years, then started building his own drive-in just northeast of the Hudson city limits. After a preview for invited guests the night before, the official grand opening of the Corral was April 25, 1952, according to a note printed in the

The Corral sat on a wedge of land next to the Neres Canal, as (barely) seen in this USGS photo taken in Sept. 1953.

following week's *Fort Lupton Press*. Mayor Fred Willmer "pushed the switch for the opening ceremony." It was the only movie theater operating in tiny Hudson.

In 1953, the Corral opened for another season, starting with long weekends in May before weeklong operation in the summer. It closed in November, and *Boxoffice* reported that "M. H. Philipsen is looking for a job for the winter," suggesting the drive-in wasn't all that lucrative. Indeed, *Boxoffice* wrote in 1960 that Philipsen was delaying opening that year "until he has finished his work as a supervisor for the Census Bureau."

Also in early 1960, Philipsen complained to his friends on Denver's Film Row that highway construction for the eventual I-76 was going to cut off access to the Corral, and that he was going to continue one more season. As it turned out, the highway bypassed the drive-in, but the Sept. 4, 1961 issue of *Boxoffice* reported that he was dismantling the Corral.

Ignacio

It all started as a reservation developed to lure the Utes, living mostly across the border in New Mexico. After they moved in, the Denver & Rio Grande Railway ran a track through the reservation, and in 1882 named its station there Ignacio after the chief of the Utes' Weeminuche band. The area was opened to white settlement in 1899, and entrepreneurs began the Town of Ignacio soon after. It finally incorporated in 1913.

Buckskin Drive-In

Opened: April 10, 1955

Closed: 1974?

Capacity: 300 cars

After soliciting requests for the types of movies patrons wanted to see, Glen Wittstruck opened the Buckskin two miles north of town on April 10, 1955, showing *The Last Time I Saw Paris*. The screen was 85x40 feet, and the top of the screen tower was 63 feet high. (One account said it was a huge 125 feet wide.) Hank Lieber, one of Wittstruck's partners, lived in an apartment next to the projection room and could watch the movies from his living room window.

Wittstruck, who lived in Meeker CO, must have wanted to retire from the theater business. In early 1957, he sold Meeker's indoor Rio Theatre to the town's dentist, and *Boxoffice* magazine reported that the Buckskin was on the market. Yet two years later, Wittstruck back at Denver's Film Row setting up film rentals for the start of the 1959 season.

By early 1962, Wittstruck had moved to Sarasota FL, and Keith Dunbar had moved down from Meeker to take over the Buckskin. In the summer of 1964, Dunbar sold it to Garland Smith and returned to Meeker, where he was soon elected Rio

The Buckskin sat on an odd bit of land, bounded by Dry Creek Ditch to the west and Highway 172 to the east. © Historicaerials.com, used by permission.

Blanco County judge. From that point, the Buckskin's story trails off. An April 1971 report in *Boxoffice* said that newcomer Jack Murphy was reopening the Buckskin "which had been closed for the past four years," and that's the last I know about it.

Although it was north of Ignacio, the Buckskin was the southernmost drive-in theater in Colorado history, beating Trinidad's Peak Drive-In by about two miles.

Julesburg

In the 1850s, Jules Beni established a way station near a ford on the South Platte River, and eventually ran it for the Leavenworth City & Pikes Peak Express stagecoach line. Those stagecoaches, especially the ones carrying valuables, kept getting robbed along the way, and Beni was forced to leave. He later got into an epic Wild West conflict against the new stationmaster, Jack Slade, whose men killed him in 1861. Monogram Pictures depicted this battle in the 1953 movie *Jack Slade*.

Julesburg / Arrow Drive-In

Opened: May 4, 1955

Closed: Aug. 2, 1969

Capacity: 368 cars

From the size of the trees to the right and all of those houses
in the back, I'd guess this photo of the Arrow was taken after
the Martenses had been running it a while. Photo courtesy
Fort Sedgwick Historical Society.

In early 1955, Herman Koeppen and Merrill Nygren
built the Julesburg Drive-In, less than two miles south of
the Nebraska border, next to a railroad overpass on the
west end of town. They combined the usual concession-
projection booth with the box office in one building at the
rear of the 318-car viewing field.

As the Julesburg's screen was first being hoisted
upright, it broke apart, delaying the opener by a few
weeks. It finally opened in May, but Nygren had to
return to Nebraska to settle his other drive-ins there.
Koeppen sold the Julesburg in August 1955 to Herb and
Doris Martens, who had been running the small airport
across the highway. They renamed it the Arrow, with a
20-foot neon arrow at the entrance.

The Martenses put in a 76-foot screen, new
projectors, and 50 more speakers, expanding the Arrow
to 368 cars. They could watch the movie from their living
room window, and they wired in a speaker to listen to

the sound system. After the death of Doris's father, they built a second house with a similar setup. One night in the early 1960s, Herb turned off the movie just long enough to let his patrons watch a satellite passing overhead. You can't do that indoors!

Business had begun to fade in 1969, and the Martenses were getting tired of running the drive-in, a farm supply store, and occasional flying lessons on the side. A severe electrical storm struck the Arrow hours after a typical Saturday night show. Lightning fried many of the speaker-post transformers, damaged the ground wire, and blasted a hole in the ground. For the Martens, that was it; they offered to sell their equipment to anyone who wanted to keep a drive-in in town, but that didn't happen.

In an ad in the *Julesburg Grit-Advocate*, the Martenses wrote, "We wish to also announce at this time that we are quitting the theatre business … We will miss you, but for physical reasons we are not able to continue operating two businesses at the same time. We feel we can't do justice to either, so we will try to do the best we can with one." The Arrow was dismantled the following spring.

La Jara

La Jara has always been a small town, tucked away in the southern part of the San Luis Valley. The US Census showed 912 residents in 1950, and although that was the highest number recorded, the population has typically stayed not that far from 800. Its Town Hall is the old two-story railroad depot, built in 1911 for the Denver and Rio Grande Railroad.

Roundup Drive-In

Opened: July? 1953

Closed: 1971?

Capacity: 300 cars

Most small local newspapers got excited about the prospect of a drive-in theater opening in town. Not the *La Jara Gazette*. There were no full-page splashes or breathless announcements for the Roundup Drive-In in the summer of 1953. Its first ad, in the Aug. 6 issue, wasn't for a grand opening; it just listed the movies on tap for the week the starting the following Tuesday. Folks there just knew to drive a mile north of town to watch.

On the other hand, *Boxoffice* gave its readers a play-by-play of the Roundup's progress. The magazine noted on Sept. 27, 1952 that the 300-car drive-in was already under construction north of La Jara. On April 18, it projected the opener for May 1. The July 4 issue of *Boxoffice* finally reported, "Mr. and Mrs. Herb Gumper opened their new Roundup Drive-In Theatre by inviting the public to a free show." Despite that past-tense pronouncement, it's possible that the opening night slipped again, but July is a good guess.

In its first ad, in the Aug. 4, 1953 issue of the *La Jara Gazette*, the Roundup stayed tight with the indoor La Jara Theater, also owned by Herbert Gumper.

If you've been reading this book front-to-back, you might recognize the Roundup's owner. Herbert Gumper owned the indoor La Jara Theatre and a store in La Jara, and two years after the Roundup's apparent success, he built the Frontier Drive-In in Center. He still owned both drive-ins when he died of a heart attack while on a fishing trip in July 1964.

Herbert's son Max took over the Roundup, keeping it running for about another decade. *Boxoffice* reported that he installed a new marquee before the 1971 season, so we know it was open then, but the *Gazette* didn't include any ads for it in the summer of 1972.

La Junta

It may be unfair to the city of La Junta, which is the seat of Otero County, but I always think of Bent's Old Fort when I think of this place. It sits at "the junction" (English for La Junta) of the mountain fork of the Santa Fe Trail and a trade route to Mexico. William and Charles Bent built the fort, more of a trading post, in 1833. In 1849, William destroyed the fort, but in 1960, an excellent reconstruction opened up as a National Historic Site.

La Junta Drive-In

Opened: Sept. 22, 1948

Closed: 1981?

Capacity: 350 cars

I wonder what was going on in Dodge City KS. In July 1948, *Boxoffice* reported that a guy from Dodge City was going to build a drive-in west of La Junta, but that didn't happen. One month later, the magazine said that two other guys from Dodge City, William Barton and Dr.

Clair Alderson, were building a drive-in two miles east of town. That one became the La Junta Drive-In, which opened in September.

Barton moved to town to run the drive-in, which had a 56x54-foot screen and could hold 350 cars. Alderson, a physician, remained in Dodge City to run his private practice there.

In 1950, local grocer Basil Smith bought Barton's share of the La Junta. Dr. Alderson retained his share, at least at the time. It's unclear whether Alderson later sold out or stayed a silent partner for decades to come. Barton went off to build the Senator Drive-In in Prescott AZ.

Smith was definitely the guy in charge in the 1950s. In 1951, he let all junior high and high school students in effectively for free (just the 8-cent tax) to see *The Jackie Robinson Story*. On one "Buck Night" in 1953, he let a busload of 40 Boy Scouts see a movie for just $1. Smith also acquired the town's indoor theater that year when Fox had to unload it to satisfy an anti-monopoly consent decree.

Commonwealth Theatres bought both of La Junta's theaters in the early 1970s and installed Roger Sargent as manager of the drive-in. In 1974, Sargent held an *Old Yeller* look-alike contest in conjunction with a showing of the film. In 1975, he admitted the driver of any 1962 Chevrolet free to watch *American Graffiti* while encouraging local radio stations to play songs from the 1960s.

This 1964 photo showed a pattern of light-colored dust, as from a graveled field. Most patrons turned west when they left, heading back to town. © Historicaerials.com, used by permission.

In early 1977, the same storm that destroyed the screen tower in nearby Rocky Ford also damaged La Junta's. The drive-in rebuilt and was showing movies later that summer, but the La Junta didn't last many more seasons. By 1982, its ads had disappeared from the *La Junta Tribune-Democrat*.

Lakewood

This doesn't happen often, but it's a little awkward. When both of the following drive-ins opened, Lakewood didn't technically exist. It was more of a neighborhood with that name; Lakewood relied on Jefferson County for law enforcement and haphazard street light and sidewalk placement. In 1969, it incorporated as Jefferson City, but the residents soon realized the possible confusion with the capitol of Missouri, so another election fixed that.

West Drive-In

Opened: July 17, 1948

Closed: Oct. 2, 1986

Capacity: 750 cars

The drive-in that would become the East hadn't even opened yet in June 1947 when John Wolfberg acquired the land for his company's second drive-in at 6th Avenue and Kipling Street. Construction on the West started the following spring.

The West started with a 70-foot steel screen with a free playground in front. (By August, it had added a pony

By 1971, housing had surrounded the West. © Historicaerials.com, used by permission.

The West sign stood along Kipling Street north of 6th Avenue. 1984 photo by Kenneth James Mitchell.

ride.) The lot held almost 800 cars, and "moonlight" bulbs on 90-foot poles provided safe illumination without affecting the movie.

Concession stands were an afterthought in many of the earliest drive-ins, and Wolfberg contracted out the West's when it opened. Lem Lee sold his share of the indoor Arvada to his partners in May 1948 so he could run both the East's concession stand and this one. Lee would soon build drive-ins of his own.

Just before the drive-in opened, the *Denver Post* ran a silly short article claiming that phone calls had been pouring in to Wolfberg's office urging the company to rename the drive-in to align with a story line then appearing in the Dick Tracy comic strip. A Wolfberg spokesman patiently explained that the West sign was already built, but maybe it would name one of its future

Over 30 years after the West closed, dozens of speaker poles still littered the old viewing field. 2019 photo by the author.

drive-ins "Acres O'Riley's Acres," if the demand continued.

On June 3, 1949, the West co-hosted the world premiere of *Colorado Territory*. The week before, it called out for horses and their riders to attend the premiere to make the scene more appealing for newspaper photographers. One of the movie's stars, Virginia Mayo, appeared in person at the West in between appearances at the indoor Broadway.

That's about it. In November 1960, the West added Bernz-O-Matic in-car heaters so it could stay open all winter, just like Wolfberg's Valley and Monaco. In 1979, Commonwealth took over the Wolfberg chain, and the West closed after the 1986 season. The screen is long gone, but the ramps and many of the speaker poles are still there today.

West Colfax Drive-In

Opened: June 14, 1967

Closed: Nov. 1, 1981

Capacity: 1000 cars

Highland Theatres had wanted to build a drive-in on the west side of the Denver area for years, but the problem was that its land was across the street from the Lakewood fire station. The solution they finally worked out was that the West Colfax Drive-In would not be accessible from West Colfax Avenue, but from 17th Avenue instead.

Lakewood's Mel Glatz designed the 1000-car drive-in, which had a soft opening a week before its Grand Opening on June 21, 1967. The concession stand and rest rooms ("lounges") had piped-in music, and the owners claimed that those lounges were "comparable to those of indoor theatre lounges." The two-story building faced a 100x50-foot screen tower.

A few months later, that building faced a different screen tower. Winds knocked down the original in December 1967.

Both the drive-in's sign and its newspaper ads called it the "W. Colfax," referring to the avenue

In its large grand opening ad in the *Denver Post*, the drive-in didn't spell out "West," using "W." instead, same as its "W. Colfax" sign.

behind it. By 1970, its ads called it simply the Colfax, which might have been a way to distance itself from Wolfberg's competing Compass drive-in chain. That's the way the Colfax stayed for the rest of its life. The drive-in's owner changed from Highland to Cooper Highland to Commonwealth (ironically joining the Compass group at that point), which owned it when the Colfax (or W. Colfax) closed after the 1981 season. A large grocery store occupies the site today.

1971 aerial photo. © Historicaerials.com, used by permission.

Lamar

Amos Black owned a large cattle ranch where the Santa Fe railroad built a wood depot. Black didn't want a town established on his land, so in 1886, local entrepreneurs shipped the depot and all of its associated buildings and their foundation stones three miles west of its old location. The new town was named for Lucius Quintus Cincinnatus Lamar, the secretary of the interior under President Grover Cleveland.

Arrow Drive-In

Opened: June 22, 1973

Closed: 1981?

Capacity: 350 cars

In the summer of 1969, Loveland-based Evergreen Theatres opened the indoor Century Theatre across the street from the Lamar post office. At the time, Evergreen also announced that it would soon begin building a drive-in, effectively replacing the burnt-out Kar-Vu, on the south side of town on US 287.

I don't know what happened to that south location, but after a delay of three years, Evergreen opened the Arrow on the north side of Lamar, on US 50/287 just after the highway

The Arrow's grand opening ad promised potted plants for the ladies.

turns west. Vern Peterson and John Lindsey, who built the Pines a few years earlier, stuck around to operate the Arrow. They left in January 1977, when Dan Wolfenbarger of Dumas TX bought the Arrow and the Century from Evergreen. Peterson and Lindsey said they would shift their attention to their Loveland theaters.

Before the 1979 season, Wolfenbarger passed the Arrow and the Century along to Stan Dewsnup, who owned Delta's drive-ins and had revived Craig's just a few years earlier. By 1982, the Arrow had stopped advertising in the *Lamar Tri-State Daily News*. An automobile scrap yard occupies the site today.

Kar-Vu Drive-In

Opened: May 25, 1950

Closed: September 1962

Capacity: 400 cars

The Atlas Theatres Corp., led by Charles "C. U." Yaeger, announced in the summer of 1949 that it would build a small drive-in in Lamar. By the time construction began in the spring of 1950, the drive-in had grown to medium size, with a 400-car viewing field.

This ad was premature. The real grand opening was pushed back a week.

The Kar-Vu was about two miles east of downtown Lamar on the south side of US 50, north of the Lamar Canal. Its screen faced southeast, away from the highway. Atlas delayed its opening for a week to complete surfacing the field and add concession stand equipment. A year later, in the summer of 1951, Atlas hired 17-year-old Fay Boyd to manage the drive-in.

The Kar-Vu's last ad in the *Lamar Tri-State Daily News* was on Sept. 13, 1962 for a "Spanish night." The Kar-Vu would typically advertise Spanish-language movies several weeknights per month. In April 1963, *Boxoffice* reported that the Kar-Vu had been damaged by fire over the winter and would remain closed. Well over 50 years later, some of the Kar-Vu's ramps are still faintly visible in aerial photos, and its old thin wooden gateway still stands.

Littleton

Richard Little was an engineer hired to lay out canals south of Denver. He fell in love with the place and brought his wife over in 1862 to start a farm. With some neighbors, the Littles built the Rough and Ready Flour

Mill in 1867. Then the Denver and Rio Grande Railroad arrived in 1871, the Littles subdivided their property into a village. Long story short, its 245 residents voted in 1890 to incorporate the Town of Littleton.

Centennial Drive-In

Opened: April 17, 1954

Closed: Oct. 24, 1976

Capacity: 1250 cars

In 1953, the Centennial Turf Club had an idea about expanding its profitable horse racing track in Littleton into other ventures. It planned a skating rink, dance hall, TV studio, and yes, a twin-screen drive-in theater. Television Theatres leased the land, and after they beat a zoning challenge from the South Drive-In, veteran drive-in builder Tom Griffing got to work.

The Centennial's screens were 100x67 feet each, facing north and south across a symmetrical viewing field. Stereo in-car speakers provided unusually good

Motion Picture Herald published this aerial photo, taken when construction on the Centennial was almost complete. The playground area next to the center projection / concession building was still without equipment.

sound quality. The elaborate children's playground had the usual features plus a miniature train. Zero's Hollywood Circus tent, run by the diminutive Mr. Zero, featured cartoons and car rides. In all, the drive-in cost $500,000 to build.

Boxoffice covered the Centennial's ribbon cutting. These four men (L to R) were Ralph Batschelet, Littleton mayor Norman Grannes, *The Robe* star Jay Robinson, and drive-in manager Robert Demshki.

The drive-in's owners hoped that it would make a natural complement to the track next door, which only operated during the day and would advertise each night's movies during the racing program. They hired veteran Denver-area theater man Ralph Batschelet as vice-president and general manager of Television Theatres to manage the drive-in at its heavily promoted grand opening. The Centennial's first movie was *The Robe*, a CinemaScope blockbuster that was one of the first films with a stereo soundtrack.

From all accounts, Batschelet gave his all in promoting the Centennial. He gave away thousands of prizes, including a car, during its first few weeks. In July, he brought in an aerial act to perform at intermission. In August, he tried Lucky Seven nights, with every car that had a license plate with a seven getting in free. The Centennial closed for the season in November.

When Batschelet resigned in February 1955 to "enter other businesses," that was a sign of trouble; indeed, his old drive-in failed to open that spring. In May, Lee Theatres, which already had the Wadsworth and the Monaco, bought the Centennial for the bargain price of

Another view of the Centennial's two screens, and the
empty fields behind them, from the 1954-55 *Theatre Catalog*.

$300,000 and reopened it with a belated first anniversary
celebration, offering five movies and five cartoons for five
cents a person.

By 1956, the race track next door was putting up
lights for night racing, making it a lot less complementary business. In 1958, Western Amusement of Los Ange-
les took over the Centennial from Lee. In December 1960,
Fox Intermountain took over the drive-in. Because it was
restrained from adding theaters at will, Fox first had to
convince a federal judge that it wouldn't affect theater
competition in the area, arguing that the Centennial's
three lessees had failed to operate it successfully.

In March 1963, a 100-mile-per-hour wind knocked
down the Centennial's north screen and did other
damage. The drive-in kept only its south screen after
that, regrading some of the north field ramps to point
south. The South Platte River flooded in 1965, covering
the field in silt up to a foot deep; workers had to truck
away over 500 tons of the stuff before reopening.

Before the 1970 season, the Centennial race track,
which always owned the land, declined to renew its lease
and took over the drive-in. By 1975, Bill Gandy was
managing the Centennial, and he added a wildly
successful Sunday flea market. It was said that some
sellers lined up at the gate immediately after the
Saturday night show to get a good spot on Sunday.

In the end, nothing could beat the money that housing and shopping center developers could offer for the land. The drive-in closed after the 1976 season, and the race track followed in November 1983.

Longmont

Longmont's origin was smart, if a bit clinical. In 1870, a bunch of folks from Chicago wanted to live in their own town in Colorado. They bought memberships, shares really, in the "Chicago-Colorado Colony." The organizers bought 60,000 acres, then brought in the members and their supplies. Even the name they chose the next year was logical, named after Long's Peak, clearly visible from their new town.

Star-Vu Drive-In

Opened: June? 1950

Closed: 1987

Capacity: 350 cars

George and Faye Barton plus Harold Bates all came up from Sharon Springs KS to build a drive-in in Longmont. It was still under construction in April 1950, and the first ad for the Star-Vu that I could find in the *Longmont Times-Call* was on June 5 that year. It didn't say anything about a grand opening, but the ad called out some benefits of the drive-in, such as "a screen as big as all outdoors" and "no

The Star-Vu's first newspaper ad.

The Star-Vu's neon stars blinked. I wonder whether the "ar" above blinked too, or whether that part of the sign was just out of order. 1980 photo © Steve Fitch, used by permission.

walking." The location was "¼ mile west of Johnson's North Station on the Hygiene Road," which today I'd call 17th Avenue about a half mile west of US 287.

The owners hired Robert Jones to manage the Star-Vu. It held 350 cars and had a screen facing northwest.

Just a year later in June 1951, Denver residents Mr. and Mrs. Merle Swank, who owned the indoor Nova in Stockton KS, and Don Phillips of Colby KS got together and bought the Star-Vu from its original owners. In 1953, the Swanks and Phillips bought the McCook NE drive-in as well.

Before the 1958 season, it was Carl Halberg's turn to own the Star-Vu after buying it from the Swanks-Phillips group. (**Crossover alert:** As detailed in my 2019 book

Drive-Ins of Route 66, Halberg also owned the Sunset in Albuquerque NM around the same time.) Then Richard Klein took over before the 1963 season, and that was the end of the ownership merry-go-round.

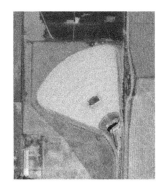

In 1971, the Star-Vu was still amid open fields. © Historic-aerials.com, used by permission.

Klein, who had already owned the indoor Trojan in Longmont, settled in for major improvements at the Star-Vu, replacing equipment and refurbishing the grounds. The drive-in's marquee had stars that blinked; I'm not sure whether Klein inherited those stars or added that touch.

In 1986, after losing money for a couple of years, Klein leased the Star-Vu to Commonwealth Theatres, though that arrangement also lasted only a couple of years. The drive-in closed for good after the 1987 season, and its screen was dismantled the following spring. A housing development sits in its place today.

Louisville

The Welch Mine, the region's first coal mine, opened in August 1877. Nearby landowner Louis Nawatny divided his farm into a town, which of course he named after himself. The town incorporated on June 3, 1882. It had a few tumultuous decades of mine owners vs. workers, but settled down quite a bit after the mines closed in the 1950s. Today multiple magazines include Louisville on their lists of best places to live in the US.

L&L Motor Vu / Star-Lite Drive-In

Opened: May 15, 1953

Closed: October 1980

Capacity: 225 cars

Carmen Romano, owner of the indoor Rex in Louisville, and Walter Houser, owner of the indoor La-Fay in Lafayette, collaborated in 1952 to build a drive-in between their two towns. After nearly a year of construction, the L&L Motor Vu opened to the public on May 15, 1953. Although it was sometimes described as halfway to Lafayette, the drive-in was barely east of the Louisville city limits on South Boulder Road.

Since it was closer to Romano's home, it's no surprise that he was the one who ran the L&L Motor Vu. In the 1950s and 60s, the drive-in attracted patrons from Boulder as well as its L&L towns. Before the 1971 season, Romano and Houser sold it to Daryl Decker, also from Louisville. A couple of years later, Decker added the Rex when Carmen and Ann Romano retired.

In late 1975, Lafayette sort of struck back. MSB Associates, based there, took over the L&L Motor Vu, the Rex, and the indoor Lamar in Lamar. Before the 1979 season, Richard Bateman's Theatre Services and Management began operating the drive-in. At the time, it announced that it would be renamed the Star-Lite and would sell admission by

The L&L Motor Vu's humble grand opening ad.

the carload. The 1980 season opener ad in the *Louisville Times* still called it to L&L, but by June 18, it switched to the Star Lite, "formerly the L&L Drive-In".

The Star-Lite didn't advertise in 1981, so the end of the 1980 season was probably the end of the drive-in. Subsequent stories in the *Times* about redeveloping the site always called it the former L&L or L&L Motor Vu. A veterinarian's office had occupied the former entrance for over 25 years, but the L&L's ramps were still visible as recently as 2015. Freshly built housing has since covered the old drive-in viewing field.

Loveland

This city, founded in 1877 next to a new line of the Colorado Central Railroad, was named for William Loveland, the railroad's president. (Loveland Pass, near the Eisenhower Tunnel, was also named after that guy, but it's nowhere near Loveland the city.) Loveland sits directly south of Fort Collins, and the two cities have been creeping toward each other as they grew. The next drive-in in our list was almost halfway between those two cities.

Pines Drive-In

Opened: June 8, 1967

Closed: 1984

Capacity: 500 cars

In May 1965, Vern Peterson was Loveland's local manager for the Commonwealth Theatres chain, which had expanded into Colorado just a couple of years earlier by purchasing the indoor Rialto there. That's when Peterson bought the Rialto and formed Evergreen

The Pines sign had deteriorated but was still hanging in
there in this 1990 photo published in the Fort Collins *Triangle
Review*. Photo courtesy Fort Collins Museum of Discovery,
T00213.

Theatres, Inc., with John Lindsey. Peterson announced
that Evergreen would build a drive-in three miles north
of town on US 287. It would effectively replace the
Motorena, which had closed a few years earlier.

I don't know what caused the delay, but
construction didn't begin on the Pines until the spring of
1967. In its Grand Opening ad, the owners proclaimed
that "your car is your castle at the outdoor theatre." The
Loveland Daily Reporter-Herald reported that the drive-in
had "a giant 460,000-inch screen." That's one way to
make the numbers look big; after doing the math, I'd
guess that translated to 80x40 feet. The Pines also had a
lighted playground.

And that's most of the story. After expanding for a
few years in the 1970s in Lamar, Evergreen sold its extra

theaters and concentrated on Loveland. By 1982, Terri Stoner was running a weekend flea market at the Pines. After the 1984 season, the drive-in closed and faded away. Storage units occupy the site today.

Luv-Vu / Motorena Drive-In

Opened: June 1, 1951

Closed: 1963?

Capacity: 300 cars

Elmer Martell came down to Loveland from Billings MT in late 1950, eager to jump on the drive-in bandwagon. But the Korean War and the National Production Authority paused Martell's plans until he could get an NPA construction permit. Work started in the spring of 1951.

The Luv-Vu opened at 14th Street and US 287, in a neighborhood known as Kings Corner. It had a 50x55-foot screen tower enclosing a 32x44-foot screen. Neon signs indicated its entrance and exit, as well as an attraction board at the entrance. Elmer's brother Eldon Martell and his family ran the drive-in.

Free popcorn and more in the grand opening ad for the Luv-Vu.

In August, floods covered the Luv-Vu in mud. The drive-in had to close down for a few days, but the equipment in the projection room escaped damage.

In November 1951, Richard Koenig, owner of Boulder's Motorena, bought the Luv-Vu from Elmer Martell. Koenig soon renamed his new acquisition, also calling it the Motorena. I guess once you've created a trademark, you just want to keep using it. That spring Koenig refurbished Loveland's Motorena, giving it a new boxoffice, signs (of course), and a new fence.

In 1957, Gibralter Theatres announced that it would renovate Loveland's indoor Rialto and the Motorena. The drive-in got a new all-metal screen tower supporting a wider MagnaVision screen, new parking ramps and a revamped sound system.

By 1964, the indoor Rialto was advertising in the *Loveland Daily Reporter-Herald*, but the Motorena had stopped. The drive-in was completely gone by a 1969 aerial photo. An assortment of retail shops are there today.

Intermission: False Alarms

Nothing beats contemporary sources when researching drive-in theaters ... most of the time. Every so often, those overworked writers at movie trade publications repeated what they read about nearby drive-ins without noticing that the original newspaper stories that they were summarizing were about drive-in restaurants. That happened at least four times in Colorado. I hate to complain, but I had to chase down each of these "leads" to verify that they weren't about the kind of drive-ins we really care about. Here are the direct quotes:

"One of the West's most beautiful Drive-In Restaurants" was Garth's in Colorado Springs, if you believe the the back of this late-1950s postcard. Since I couldn't find a good picture of any of these False Alarms, this at least shows what I mean.

Holly: Pinky's (two sources!)

Boxoffice, Aug. 6, 1950: Mr. and Mrs. LeRoy Randle have transferred their interests in Pinky's Drive-In here to John Randle and Dale Dodnil, who now are operating the open-air theatre.

Theatre Catalog, 1952 and 1953-54 editions: Holly, Colo., Pinkys D. I., Exec: John Randle and Dale Dodnil. (Oddly enough, the car capacity was left blank.)

Englewood: the Rooster

Boxoffice, Nov. 18, 1950: A dining room has been added to the Rooster Drive-In, owned and operated by Jerry Doughty. A 15x30-foot addition was made at the front of the concession building with space for 50 customers.

Arvada, the Hillcrest (twice!)

Boxoffice, June 16, 1951: Ernest R. Bacher and I. J. Bacher staged a first anniversary birthday party at their Hillcrest Drive-In and issued a blanket invitation to the public to attend. To show their appreciation to the patrons who made the ozoner's first year an outstanding success, the Bachers "threw open" the doors ... and provided free fountain service from 11 a.m. to 4:30 p.m.

Boxoffice, May 31, 1952: The Hillcrest Drive-In held open house when owners Ernest and I. J. Bacher celebrated its second anniversary in May. The public was invited and flowers were given the women while free cigars were distributed to the men.

Windsor, the Valley

Boxoffice, July 21, 1969: The Valley Drive-In had a highly successful grand opening, according to manager Tom Nail. Signing the register were 1,703 visitors from 15 different states, most distant being New Hampshire and Washington. Several hundred gallons of root beer were given away, Nail said. (It was a former Dog N Suds.)

Minturn

The tiny town of Minturn was built as a rail crossroads; it was named after its founder, a vice president of the Denver and Rio Grande Western Railroad. It's never held as many as 1500 residents, though its weekly farmers market can see several times that number in the summer. Those visitors can use America's Best Public Restroom, winner of a 2015 national contest, which is located one block east of US 24 on Toledo Avenue.

Blue Starlite Mini Urban Drive-In

Opened: July 6, 2016

~~**Closed:**~~ active!

Capacity: 40 cars

Paradoxically, if you want to get an idea of what the oldest improvised rural drive-in theaters were like, the best way would be to visit one of the newest, the Blue Starlite. Every summer since 2016, it has set up shop in Little Beach Park in Minturn with a temporary screen, a small digital projector (think DVDs and USB sticks), FM stereo sound, and truck-based munchies. Visualize a vintage 16mm projector and a couple of loudspeakers in that scene, and it's pretty easy to pretend you're 70 years in the past.

The Blue Starlite's "ticket booth" is a bucket on a stepstool, and those speakers are mainly for show, since its movies use FM stereo sound. 2017 photo by the author.

Josh Frank started the Blue Starlite, a "mini, artisanal" drive-in, in suburban Austin TX on July 4, 2012. A few years later, he must have recognized that summers in the Colorado mountains are much more pleasant than summers in central Texas, so every year, he brings his equipment back to Minturn.

Local food trucks replace the traditional concession stand, the Eagle River flows just out of sight, and mini lights and a s'mores-ready fire pit complement the ambience. Frank calls Minturn's Blue Starlite the "highest" drive-in in America. I once mentioned to him that Buena Vista's Comanche is almost 8000 feet up, about 100 more than his drive-in. He said he already knew that.

Monte Vista

It all started with a water tank, plus all the other parts of a water station, laid out by the Denver & Rio Grande Railroad. In 1882, Lillian L. Fassett set up a small general store nearby, and homesteaders soon followed. Short-term promoter Theodore Henry set up a town there, but after he left in a hurry, the folks still holding the pieces renamed it from Henry to Monte Vista in 1886.

Star Drive-In

Opened: July 1, 1955

~~**Closed:**~~ active!

Capacity: 300 cars

The Kelloffs were one of the first theater families in Colorado. Najib Kelloff (also spelled Nagib, Nagept, Nashep and Najeeb, maybe he had a thick accent) was an immigrant from Lebanon who owned the Ute Theatre

Except for adding an electronic sign, Monte Vista's Star looks about the same today as it did in this 1997 photo by the author.

There's nothing else like sitting in a motel room and looking out at a movie on a drive-in screen. 2004 photo © Captus Lumen Photography, used by permission.

(and a grocery store) in tiny Aguilar. One of his sons, Mitchell, ran the Uptown in Pueblo. Our story is about his youngest son, George.

George Kelloff was running the Ute for his dad when he married Edna Mae in 1950. Five years later, he and the wife moved to Monte Vista to build his drive-in a couple of miles west of town. George erected the Star on the site of an old airport. An avid pilot, he maintained some of the runways for years afterward. The new drive-in held 500 cars, and the Kelloffs lived in an apartment, complete with movie speaker, in the projection building.

In early 1962, Edna's parents came to visit, and George let them use the bedroom while he and Edna slept on the living room sofa bed. Michael Karl Witzel described the resulting eureka moment in his book *The American Motel*: "From their vantage point on that tiny guest bed, they both realized that they could watch the movie – right through the picture window that faced out toward the drive-in screen! … Energized by his new discovery, he was convinced that 'people would pay to lay in bed and watch a movie.' "

So in 1964, George built a 14-unit motel with the rooms wired for movie sound. He added a restaurant and lounge the following spring, and doubled the size of the motel with a second floor in 1967. The Movie Manor would eventually grow to 60 rooms.

At the turn of the millennium, George added a second screen to the Star. It uses a separate, smaller projection hut, and is more difficult to see from most rooms, but since it's on FM radio sound, listening to the movies there is still possible.

In 2012, George upgraded both screens to digital projection. The next year, he sold the Movie Manor to Mike Suthar and retired to Arizona.

George wasn't the first person to build a motel with a view of a drive-in. In 1960, a couple in Fairlee VT added six rooms behind their snack bar. Over 90% of drive-ins active since then have closed. It's a testament to the power of these complementary businesses that both the Star and the Fairlee continue operating today.

Montrose

Montrose was named after a fictional character, the hero of a novel by Sir Walter Scott that founder Joseph Selig must have really liked. In 1909, the Gunnison Tunnel irrigated the Uncompahgre Valley with Gunnison River water, making Montrose part of an agricultural center. Now it's the closest city to the Black Canyon of the Gunnison National Park.

Star Drive-In

Opened: April 19, 1950

~~Closed:~~ active!

Capacity: 360 cars

In 1949, Henry Barrett of Cedaredge and George DeVries of Olathe started building the Star east of Montrose on what was then the cemetery road. When it opened the following spring, the Star had a 60x50-foot screen and was managed by Barrett. Before the 1952 season, DeVries bought out his partner's share, (reportedly owned by Mr. and Mrs. Otis Millard at that point), and his family has owned it ever since.

According to *Boxoffice*, DeVries leased the Star to a Delta drive-in operator at least a couple of times. Max Story, who ran the Skylite, leased the Star in 1952. Stan

The sign at Montrose's Star stands in front of its screen, which was erected in 1974. 1998 photo by the author.

One year later, the Star's sign had changed a little, but most everything else stayed the same. 1999 photo by the author.

Dewsnup, already operating both Delta drive-ins, temporarily added the Star in 1977. They were two minor notes in a mostly quiet, single-family history.

In March 1960, DeVries had to postpone the season opener because the snow was too deep for even four-wheel drive vehicles to get in. On May 19, 1974, a twister or wind gust destroyed the screen. The manager then was DeVries's daughter Pamela, who had taken over a few years earlier. They reopened 10 days later with an 80x86-foot screen. Later, pointing to a photo of the wreckage, Pamela told Grand Junction's *Daily Sentinel*, "That tornado took down the original screen. We only had $12,000 in insurance. It cost $25,000 to replace."

When DeVries passed away in 1995, the Star passed to Pamela Friend and her siblings. She says that her mother frequently ran the place during the early years, while her father did the book work. By age 5, Pamela was running tickets from the booth to the projection room, and she was running the Star as a teenager.

In 2012, Pamela organized a "Save the Star" fundraiser for a digital projector. That raised about $24,000; she took out a loan on the family farm to raise the rest of the cost of the upgrade. Today potatoes, tomatoes and onions from that farm find their way to the concession stand as fresh-cut French fries and burger condiments.

Pamela Friend boasts that the Star is the oldest drive-in that's still owned and operated by the family that built it. She's probably right.

Naturita

Naturita was part of the Uravan Mineral Belt, which supplied the uranium for the world's first atomic bombs. The area's big boom (excuse the pun) came when workers and their families streamed in to harvest the mineral. The price of uranium plummeted around 1980, and the resulting mining bust hit the area hard. Today, the town is recovering. The Naturita Community Library, housed in a geothermal building made of straw bales, received the "Best of Small Libraries in America" award in 2011.

Uranium Drive-In

Opened: March 13, 1954

Closed: 1984?

Capacity: 275

The restored Uranium sign was moved to the middle of Naturita, whose leaders use its message board for public service announcements. 2019 photo by the author.

William Moore financed the construction of Naturita's first theater, the Uranium, built on the road to Nucla. It was built by Ted Knox, a regional drive-in equipment supplier, and a local assistant, Paul Campbell. At the end of its first season, Moore widened the screen to accommodate CinemaScope.

In 1957, Moore wanted to enlarge the Uranium, but the state highway department had the opposite idea. It straightened Highway 97, carving off a small slice of the back of the drive-in's viewing field.

Then in 1959, things got weird. Moore bought and moved (!) the Starlite from one side of Grand Junction to the other. (More about that in the Starlite's chapter.) Not only did Clarence Files quickly buy back the Starlite, but in 1960, Files also acquired the Uranium from Moore.

That must have been one heck of a story, or a Hollywood poker game bet, or something mundane like putting up the Uranium as collateral for a loan to buy the Starlite.

Clarence and June Files ran the Uranium until the summer of 1967, when they sold it to Jay and Kathryn Randolph. In 1976, Laurence Stieb bought the Uranium from the Randolphs, and that's the last bit of information I have about this drive-in.

Exactly when did the Uranium close? A March 1983 *Christian Science Monitor* story mentioned it in passing, but a 1986 photo by Robert Dawson showed the marquee already in disrepair. In any event, the city of Naturita acquired the original sign, restored it, and moved it to the center of town in 2012. It's still there today. In 2013, Suzan Beraza released a documentary about the possible return of uranium mining and called it *Uranium Drive-In*.

Norwood

Harry Copp came to Wright's Mesa in 1885 and formed a town, becoming its first mayor and postmaster. He named it Norwood after his home town in Missouri. It's always been small, only recently nudging above 500 residents, so it fits that Norwood hosted what was then the smallest drive-in in the state.

Norwood Drive-In

Opened: 1952?

Closed: 1974?

Capacity: 62 cars

Of all the drive-ins in this book, my information on this one is the sketchiest. I couldn't find any mentions in newspapers or trade publications. So let me build this story from the bones that I could find.

A tiny drive-in showed up just east of Norwood on state highway 145 in a July 1952 USGS aerial photo. The viewing field was roughly 85,000 square feet. (To compare, the average-sized field at the Star in Montrose is about 250,000 square feet.) It first appeared in the *Theatre Catalog* in its 1953-54 edition as the Norwood Drive-In, capacity 62 cars, owner F. H. Buss.

The tiny Norwood looked intact, north of the highway, in 1963. © Historic-aerials.com, used by permission

That would be Fred H. Buss, who moved to Norwood in 1927. Grand Junction's *Daily Sentinel* wrote that Buss "engaged in ranching and livestock raising until his retirement." One of Fred's sons was Boyd Buss, and the 1940 federal census listed Boyd's occupation as "Motion picture theater owner". Boyd's obituary would later say that he "operated the theaters in Norwood".

Fred passed away suddenly in March 1957. I would guess that Boyd took over the drive-in along with running the indoor Mesa Theatre in town. The Mesa was also tiny, seating 175.

For clues to the end of the Norwood's life, we turn to the often-fallible *Motion Picture Almanac*. The drive-in's first appearance there was its 1953-54 edition, where it was called the T. A. Buss Drive-In, owner T. A. Buss, capacity 64 cars. I've read about a lot of Busses, but I haven't found one yet with those initials. In its 1956 edition, the *Almanac* changed the drive-in's name to Norwood, but it persisted with T. A. as the owner for the rest of its run. The *Almanac* included the Norwood through the 1967-76 decade when it was printing its drive-in list mostly on autopilot. When the *Almanac* rebooted that list for its 1977 edition, the Norwood was gone.

The last aerial photo of the Norwood was in 1965, when it showed a slightly larger screen and a slightly larger projection booth. The drive-in was still outlined on a 1968 topo map, but in a September 1978 photo it was long gone, a house built near its old entrance.

Paonia

Samuel Wade settled here in 1880, and he named the town Paeonia, part of the Latin name for the peony. (Wade brought some peony roots with him from Ohio.) The post office simplified the name to Paonia. Although cattle and sheep ranchers soon followed, I think of the Paonia area as a great place for growing fruit.

Paonia Drive-In

Opened: June 7, 1957

Closed: Aug. 30, 1987

Capacity: 300

The owner of the indoor Paonia Theatre, Tom Poulos, began building a drive-in west of town on state highway 135 in the spring of 1957. Staying on theme, Poulos named his new showcase the Paonia Drive-In. It

Although little else of the drive-in remains, the Paonia's sign still looks great today. 2019 photo by the author.

opened on schedule on June 7 that year even though some of its equipment hadn't arrived.

The Paonia had 260 speakers and a small, wide screen, 34 feet by 78 feet. Tom's son Don managed the drive-in as well as the indoor Paonia.

In 1964, Tom's health began to fade, and his son-in-law, Robert Musgrave of Hotchkiss, leased the Paonia for a season. The following winter, Delta County clerk Homer Graham took over for at least the 1965 season. Tom passed away at the age of 77 in early 1966.

At some point, Musgrave must have purchased both Paonia theaters, probably from the Poulos estate. He reopened the indoor Paonia in December 1968 and was mentioned as the drive-in's owner in 1970.

Dominic Linza, who ran the indoor Isis in Aspen, acquired the Paonia before the 1973 season from Mrs.

"Stevie" Musgrave. And the drive-in continued operating well into the 1980s. Its final ad in the *North Folk Times* was in the Aug. 27, 1987 edition. The following summer, the drive-in's ads were gone.

Pueblo

Today's Pueblo was formed over a century ago by merging the original Pueblo, South Pueblo, Central Pueblo, and Bessemer. My favorite event in the city is the Colorado State Fair, held there every year since before Colorado was a state. The Southern Colorado Agricultural and Industrial Association held its first three-day fair north of Pueblo in 1872.

Hicks / 96 / East Drive-In

Opened: June 12, 1953

Closed: Sept. 3, 1979

Capacity: 360

Although this drive-in of many names is Pueblo's first alphabetically using any of them, it was the last of the four to open. And despite being the last to open, it was the first to close. Still, 27 seasons is a good, long run for any drive-in.

Marion J. "Dutch" Konemann was an all-star halfback at Georgia Tech. After graduation, service in World War II, and general bouncing around, he and his wife managed Dallas TX's Hi-Vue Drive-In, where he was also part owner.

In early, 1953, Konemann moved with his wife to Pueblo to build a modest-sized drive-in. According to Michael P. Thomason's book *Night Lights*, he shared ownership with his wife, Polly. At its grand opening, they advertised it as the "Hicks on '96'," referring to the landowner, grocer James Hicks, and its location on state highway 96. But every industry drive-in list called it simply the Hicks.

FOLKS! DON'T MISS
GRAND OPENING
HICKS ON "96"
DRIVE-IN MOVIES
ENTRANCE

Your East Side Drive In–Pueblo's Newest

TODAY IS THE DAY–FRIDAY–JUNE 12th
SHOW TIME 7:00 P. M. —EVERYTHING FOR YOUR
CONVENIENCE—COME AS YOU ARE—
AND SEE WHAT WE HAVE IN STORE FOR YOU.

ATTRACTION TODAY

RANDOLPH SCOTT IN
SUGARFOOT

Plus Bugs Bunny Revue
8 BUGS BUNNY CARTOONS
For Your Enjoyment

THE MANAGEMENT

Although Pueblo was going strong back then, I wonder whether it was ready to support a fourth drive-in. In the mid-1950s, there were a few signs that

Was it the Hicks, that was on Highway 96, or was the drive-in's name "Hicks on 96"? Looking at the grand opening ad, I'm not sure.

things weren't going that well. Dutch got the regional franchise for Modern Film Distributors in early 1955. Then in July 1957, Dutch married Louise Payne and moved with her to Grand Junction. The Hicks closed for a few days in December that year and reopened as the 96. I wonder if those last two sentences are related.

Polly now owned the 96, but not for all that long. In early 1958, she lost $96 to an armed robber. In April 1959, she listed the 96 for sale in *Boxoffice* magazine.

The exact capacity of this drive-in was widely disputed over the years. Industry magazines announced at its opening that it held 360 cars; so did the *Theatre Catalog*. The *Motion Picture Almanac* series started with a capacity of 450, changed it to 338, then changed again to 400. In her "For Sale" ad, Polly said it held 300.

Homer Hibbets was the next owner of the 96. Hibbets ran the drive-in for the next decade until the end of the 1969 season, when he sold it to Highland Theatres, which had purchased the Pueblo and the Lake earlier that year. Highland renamed it the East, and that was the end of the excitement. The East closed in 1979, though its sign still remains, repurposed for a church that now occupies the site.

Lake Drive-In

Opened: June 23, 1949

Closed: Sept. 5, 1988

Capacity: 500 cars

Lionel & Ruby Semon's first drive-in, soon to be called the Pueblo, must have been a huge success, because they immediately began work on Pueblo's second. The Lake, named for Lake Avenue, was slightly smaller than the first. It sat on the south side of town, across the avenue from Pueblo Greyhound Park, which opened a month after the drive-in.

The Lake's Grand Opening ad in the *Pueblo Chieftain* noted that the new drive-in had a concave screen and said that patrons would "see better, hear better" if they would "Come as you are in the family car."

The Lake looked intact, if a bit overgrown, in this 1991 photo by John Margolies.

The Semons added floodlights and extra playground equipment before the 1950 season, and later that summer, they almost started construction on another drive-in. Pueblo granted them a permit to build it just west of town on Highway 96, but they never followed through. The Mesa opened the following year, and three might have been the right number of drive-ins for Pueblo.

The next couple of decades were quietly stable, with the Semons running both the Pueblo and the Lake. Before the 1969 season, they sold their drive-ins to Highland Theatres. Lionel passed away two years later. Highland kept both drive-ins active for another 20 years, closing them both at the end of the 1988 season.

Mesa Drive-In

Opened: Aug. 17, 1951

~~Closed:~~ active!

Capacity: 750 cars

Strictly speaking, the Mesa isn't in Pueblo; it's in the census-designated place called Blende in unincorporated Pueblo County. Anyway, in the spring of 1950, Westland Theatres, owner of several indoor theaters in Pueblo and the 8th Street Drive-In in Colorado Springs, announced plans to build a 1200-car drive-in on then-US 50 just east of Blende. That put the site about 2½ miles east of downtown Pueblo.

Westland delayed construction until after the crops were harvested, explaining why it took so long for the Mesa to open. They built a second-floor projection booth above its concession stand, which also held 100 seats for walk-ins. Posts along a sidewalk from there to the playground protected pedestrians from cars along the way.

The Mesa had all that marquee room and just one screen back in 1998. Photo by the author.

Ronald "Tiny" Vaughn managed the Mesa during its early years while his wife Joye ran the concession stand. He was quite a character. In 1952, he brought in high-wire performers for pre-show entertainment. In 1962, he bought a German shepherd named Big Boy to replace the off-duty patrol officers he had been using to keep teenage rowdies in line. "It's been quieter at my theatre in the last three weeks than it has been in the last ten years," Vaughn told *Motion Picture Exhibitor*.

In early 1985, Kansas City-based Commonwealth Theatres bought Westland's properties. Commonwealth gave way to United Artists, which was ready to bulldoze the Mesa in 1994.

Enter Charles and Marianne James, two self-described hippies who had recently reopened the indoor Skyline in Cañon City. To save the Mesa, they bought it and started sprucing it up. In 1999, they shifted to FM radio sound. In 2000, the Jameses made a more radical change, adding two more screens acquired from the

By 2005, the lettering had changed and the Mesa was advertising three double features. Photo by the author.

closed Pines in Loveland and Lake Estes in Estes Park. They reconfigured the Mesa's viewing area from a single lot to three combining to hold about 750.

The Jameses still own the Mesa today, and it still shows movies on three screens. Their switch to digital projection in 2013 cost more than they'd paid for the entire drive-in two decades earlier, and now it looks like it could stay open forever.

Pueblo Drive-In

Opened: May 20, 1948

Closed: Sept. 4, 1988

Capacity: 725

Lionel Semon went to high school in Lawrence KS, attended the University of Kansas there, went into the theater business in Cimarron KS in the southwestern part of the state, and married Ruby Ardella. In July 1947, just

Looks like the original screen tower was framed by the comedy/tragedy masks, and a later CinemaScope upgrade extended it to the left. 1980 photo by John Margolies.

a few days after Colorado's first drive-in opened to overflow crowds, they announced plans to move to Pueblo and build one there.

Before the year was out, the Semons had started building on the site north of US 50 about a quarter mile west of what was then US 85. When it opened the following spring, it was named simply "Drive-In Theatre," as was common for early drive-ins. In less than a year, it was known as the Pueblo, but its sign continued to show the original name for decades to come.

Business must have been good, because the Semons quickly built a second drive-in on the south side of town. After that, the next couple of decades passed uneventfully; from the look of the screen tower, they probably widened it some time in the 1950s. Highland Theatres bought both of the Semons' drive-ins before the 1969 season, then continued to operate them for another 20 years. Highland closed both at the end of the 1988 season.

In 1994, a fire destroyed that magnificent screen tower. Today, the site is home to a big box Lowe's hardware store.

Intermission: Over the Edge

Across the U.S., drive-ins near a state line were fairly common. A theater operator would take advantage of more favorable treatment on his side of the line while appealing to a larger audience who lived on the other side.

As far as I can tell, none of the drive-ins that once lived just across Colorado's borders were built to draw cross-state traffic. How many of them there were depends on how you define "close." If you'd say "within 10 miles," there were at least four. If you're willing to stretch to 30 miles, there were at least 18. If you want to go farther, the number is larger, but you're going to have to make your own list.

Here are the nearby drive-ins that I've found so far, starting north at Wyoming and going clockwise around the state. Sadly, all of them are inactive today. Distances are from the drive-in, not its town, as the crow flies, and opening dates are sometimes a best guess.

Here is each drive-in's name and city, with its approximate distance from the Colorado border:

Wyoming

Skyline (opened 1949), Laramie, 22.5 miles
Co-owner/manager Robert Adams installed the Skyline's third screen in May 1950; Wyoming winds had destroyed his first two versions.

Symbols told the name of Cheyenne's Starlite Drive-In. 1980 photo by John Margolies.

Motor-Vu (opened 1949), Cheyenne, 10 miles
Built by Russ Dauterman, Al Knox, O. J. Hazen and Ray Davis. In the 1970s, manager Wayne Gow charged a per-vehicle rate on "Car Cram Nights."

Starlite (opened 1950), Cheyenne, 7.6 miles
The Motor-Vu Theatre Company built the Starlite. In 1977, a flash flood filled the projection booth with three feet of water, but the drive-in soon reopened.

Nebraska

Plains (opened 1951), Sidney, 8.3 miles
Local men Don Gillman and Robert Carter built the Plains in the winter of 1950-51. The Carter family operated it through 1962.

Panhandle (opened 1954), Kimball, 16.4 miles
Named for the Nebraska panhandle, this 250-car drive-in was built by Nate Eastman and some other Kimball business folks.

West 5th Street (opened 1953), Ogallala, 18.3 miles
Robert Kehr built the West 5th Street and owned it until 1967, when he sold the drive-in to Evergreen Theatres, which later built the Arrow in Lamar CO.

Kansas

Starlight (opened 1975), St. Francis, 14 miles
The Starlight (or Starlite) was owned by James Edmundson, who also built the Burlington (CO) Drive-In.

Goodland (opened 1950), Goodland, 17.1 miles
The Goodland sat at the northwest corner of old US 24 and Kansas Highway 27. Commonwealth Theatres was running it when it closed in the early 1970s.

Rancho 50 (opened 1953), Syracuse, 15.7 miles
Built on the west side of town north of US 50. Now home to an automobile junkyard, a common second life for former drive-ins.

New Mexico

85 (opened 1949), Raton, 8.2 miles
Once operated in conjunction with the indoor El Raton – one would be open when the other was closed. The 85 survived until at least 2004.

Rincon (opened 1954), Aztec, 13 miles
The Bolack Electromechanical Museum in Farmington reportedly owns some of the Rincon's old in-car speakers.

Yucca (opened 1958), Spencerville, 12 miles

The *Motion Picture Almanac* series consistently listed the Yucca under Aztec, but it was really in Spencerville, just west of Aztec.

Chief (opened 1954), Shiprock, 15 miles

George Armstrong of Cortez CO built the Chief, which he said was the first drive-in built on Indian-owned land. It survived into the 1980s.

Apache Twin (opened 1952), Farmington, 18 miles

Russell Allen and Kelly Crawford built the Apache as a single screen, then added a second in 1957.

Mesa (opened 1950), Farmington, 20 miles

The Mesa was four miles east of town, and had a 100-foot screen tower made of concrete and Oregon pine. It closed within a decade.

Valley (opened 1954), Farmington, 17 miles

Russell Allen and Kelly Crawford told *Boxoffice* that they built the Valley using lessons learned from building the Apache years earlier.

Utah

Nu Vu (opened 1954), Monticello, 17.5 miles

A very small (150-car) drive-in built just west of Monticello High School. Its screen came down in August 1980, though it may have closed years earlier.

Sunset (opened 1950), Vernal, 29 miles

In July 2013, when a fire damaged its concession building, the Sunset was the oldest active drive-in in Utah. It never reopened after the fire.

Rifle

The town of Rifle is named for Rifle Creek, which joins the Colorado River there. Rifle Creek was named for a rifle, which a surveying, possibly careless soldier left behind but later recovered on its bank. Rifles were named for the rifled grooves machined into their barrels. I think that's as far back as we can go on that. I highly recommend the signature waterfall of Rifle Falls State Park about 12 miles north of town. It's just gorgeous, especially in the spring.

Chief Drive-In

Opened: July 7, 1950

Closed: September 1963?

Capacity: 340 cars

In the winter of 1949-50, Mr. and Mrs. Fred Lind, owners of the indoor Ute Theatre in Rifle, went south for a vacation. It might have been a working vacation, because when they got back, they had plans to build a drive-in about three miles east of town on land they had purchased.

Half a year and about $40,000 later, the Chief opened. Its screen was 60 by 60 feet and weighed 12 tons. In his ads, Lind told patrons, "You can take off your shoes – no one will step on your toes." He also planned to build a ballroom just east of the screen; I can't tell whether he ever got around to that.

Fred Lind only had one season to enjoy his new drive-in. He died at home after a heart attack in December 1950. He was just 49, though he'd been in the hospital for heart problems two years earlier.

Donald Monson, Lind's son-in-law, was also a partner in the Chief, and he managed the drive-in from then on. Mrs. Lind remarried in 1952 and moved to California, and the Chief quietly rolled along.

In January 1961, Monson must have been getting tired of running the Chief. He put it up for sale and advertised that fact on its marquee. Yet he kept it for at least another three seasons. In September 1963, Monson performed his usual seasonal switchover of opening the Ute and closing the Chief. That's the last mention I could find for Rifle's drive-in.

Top and bottom of a Chief ad.

Rocky Ford

This little town on US 50 in the Arkansas River Valley is best known for its produce, especially its cantaloupes. Hot days and cool nights, along with plenty of freshly melted river water, combine for some of the sweetest melons you'll find anywhere.

Starlite / Starlight Drive-In

Opened: March 26, 1953

Closed: Sept. 26, 1976

Capacity: 427 cars

Local man Carl Downing and two brothers from Kansas, A. C. Sever and S. A. Sever, started building Rocky Ford's drive-in east of town on US 50 in the late summer of 1952. They held a special fundraiser grand opening the following March, with all ticket sales going to the Pioneer Memorial Hospital fund.

Except for the 48-foot-high screen, everything at the Starlite was painted coral and green – the fences, the box office, the snack bar walls, even the teeter-totters and slides in the playground. Sixteen chairs sat on the snack bar porch, which also had speakers. Mr. and Mrs. Roscoe Slease moved to town from Dodge City KS; Roscoe managed the drive-in, and the missus ran the snack bar.

Control of the Starlite passed to the Gibralter circuit, a loose confederation of regional theater owners, just a year or two later. In June 1956, manager Paul R. Anderson won a prize in *Motion Picture Exhibitor*'s Showmanship Sweepstakes for a citywide Loyalty Day promotion. "The program at the drive-in was on a Monday night and admission was free. The

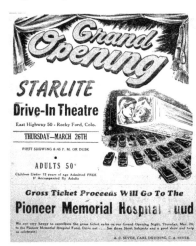

The Starlite raised $245.70 for the Pioneer Memorial Hospital Fund on opening night.

program in addition to the speeches, featured the films *Bill Of Rights* and *Men of the Fighting Lady*, and a fireworks display."

In April 1962, *Boxoffice* reported that the Starlite had been closed the year before but was widening its screen to 90 feet and painting its fence "yellow, green, tea and tangerine." That must have made it attractive, because two months later, Commonwealth Theatres of Kansas City bought the drive-in from Gibralter.

The drive-in's final ad, as the Starlight, appeared in the Sept. 24, 1976 issue of the *Rocky Ford Daily Gazette*. In April 1977, a dust storm driven by high winds destroyed its screen tower, and my guess is that Commonwealth never rebuilt it. By July 1977, the *Daily Gazette* was advertising the La Junta Drive-In, which had also been damaged by that storm, but not the Starlite/Starlight.

Salida

When the Denver and Rio Grande Railroad came through town, it was called South Arkansas after the river flowing through it. The town was renamed Salida, Spanish for "exit," to represent the gateway to the valley carved by the Arkansas River. Maybe some passengers just figured they were supposed to get off the train at that stop.

Groy / Knox Drive-In

Opened: May 12, 1950

Closed: 1958?

Capacity: 350 cars

Brothers Ben and Lewis Groy hopped on the drive-in bandwagon in early 1950, building one west of Salida on US 50. The Grand Opening was a huge success, but there were troubles soon to come.

In the summer of 1951, a windstorm or tornado blew down the screen, which bent its steel supports and toppled backwards onto the neon sign at the entrance. The Groys fixed it only after losing a full month of their busiest season.

Ted Knox, who was also running Durango's first drive-in, stepped in before the 1953 season to lease the Groy from the brothers Groy. He reopened in May that year, and in 1955 switched to advertising it as the Knox. I wish I knew whether he changed that neon sign.

In 1956, Atlas Theatres, a regional chain, took over the lease from Knox. Atlas owned the indoor Salida

Salida's drive-in started advertising as the Groy (shown in the 1953 ad on the left), then became the Knox in 1955 (center). In 1956 (right) it was just "Drive-In," but the bottom of the ad said to pick up discount tickets at the Groy Drive-In. Clippings courtesy Salida Regional Library.

Theatre and closed it for the summer while it ran the Knox. Downtown business leaders complained about the loss of foot traffic, and Atlas soon reopened the Salida even during the Knox's summer months.

Lewis's grandson John D. Groy later said the Atlas purchase was all about eliminating competition, and that description matches the record. After that 1956 season, the Knox stopped advertising in the local *Mountain Mail*. A Walmart occupies the old drive-in site today.

Sheridan

The short-lived Richard Dean Anderson TV western "Legend" was set in Sheridan, Colorado, but not this one. After Peter Magnus laid out the town of Petersburg in 1873, Isaac McBroom set up his own six-block town in 1887 and named it Sheridan Junction after Philip Sheridan, the army general who established nearby Fort Logan. When the town was incorporated in 1890, well, you can guess who won the naming contest.

Cinderella Twin Drive-In

Opened: July 18, 1973

Closed: Sept. 29, 2007

Capacity: 1000 cars

Old drive-ins theaters sometimes turn into junkyards, but not very many junkyards become drive-ins. Ken Leiman bought a junkyard just north of US 285, across the street from the Platte River, for about $1 per square foot, then leased the land to Highland Theatres. With design help from Mel Glatz of Lakewood, Highland built the Cinderella Twin, bringing Highland's local total to five screens.

The Cinderella Twin's sign was very tall so its attractions board would be at eye level for motorists on US 285 south of the drive-in. 1997 photo by the author.

After over a month of "Coming Soon" ads, the Cinderella Twin was supposed to open on July 13, but on that date, it ran a short disclaimer saying it wasn't ready yet. The metro area's only two-screen drive-in quietly opened on Wednesday, July 18, then held its official grand opening on August 8.

The Cinderella's life under corporate ownership was fairly uneventful for the next couple of decades, although those corporate owners kept changing. Highland merged with Denver-based Cooper Theatres, then Commonwealth Theatres of Kansas City MO bought out Cooper-Highland in June 1978. Commonwealth was sold to a partnership run by United Artists in 1988. And three guys who worked at the Cinderella bought the place from United Artists in March 1996.

The Cinderella Twin's last few years were always tentative, with the looming threat of losing the annual lease. 2004 photo by the author.

Jim Goble, Jeff Kohler and Ken Oborn poured their hearts into revitalizing the Cinderella, including the installation of a small playground, with four motorized rides, called Kiddieland. Goble added a bronze plaque there listing the 18 drive-ins that had existed in the Denver area. (He must have stretched that area to include Boulder, Castle Rock, or some other exurbs to reach a number that high.)

Patrons responded, keeping the Cinderella near capacity most weekends. In some summer months of 1997 and 1998, it was the most popular Denver-area theater per screen on MovieFone. But Goble knew that his drive-in's land was on borrowed time. Bruce Leiman told the *Rocky Mountain News* in June 2001, "My dad bought it around 1972 as speculation and got the wild idea to put a drive-in there. Obviously the ground's worth a lot of money, and it's getting hard to refuse."

The younger Leiman made a deal with apartment developers in July 2003, but various delays kept extending the Cinderella's life. The end finally came after the 2007 season, when Avana on the Platte Apartments' builders tore down the screens and started construction. At least they kept the old Cinderella sign, perched high above the ground to attract the attention of drivers on Hampden, though now it says "avana".

Springfield

Frank Tipton came to set up this new town, named after the city he'd just left, Springfield MO. It incorporated in 1889 and was soon made the seat of Baca County. Its first attempt at a county courthouse, a hotel from Boston CO, burned before it arrived. The next two courthouses also burned. Today's Baca County Courthouse, on Main Street across from City Hall, was built in 1929.

Sunset / Apache / Kar-Vu Drive-In

Opened: July 5, 1957

Closed: 2006?

Capacity: 350 cars

Marvin Bell and Everett Toomey, theater men from Sunray TX, came to Springfield in 1957 to build a drive-in on a hill about a mile south of town on US 287/385. Bell and Toomey had just finished building the Tab Drive-In in Phoenix the year before. Springfield's *Plainsman Herald* wrote that the new drive-in was going to be called the Sunnyside, but I'm guessing that someone there misheard; *Boxoffice* had earlier printed the correct name, the Sunset.

The drive-in featured a 70x35-foot screen tower with its back to the highway. The wide, single-story projection/concession building sat near the front of the narrow, rectangular field.

Bell and Toomey leased the Sunset in 1961 to Bob Hough and Doyle Smith of Dumas TX. The new operators added a fresh coat of paint and a fresh name, the Apache.

Despite several panels missing from its screen tower, the Kar-Vu was still showing movies in 2002. Photo by dallasmovietheaters

Before the 1964 season, Bernie Newman, owner of the indoor Gem in Walsh, bought the Apache. Newman had formed a corporation, Baca Theaters, with Ike and Ruby Ross in 1963, and the Ross family soon ran the renamed Kar-Vu.

By the 1990s, Ruby Ross was operating both the Kar-Vu and Springfield's indoor Capitol, closing one while the other was open. In 2000, she sold both to Trent and Anna High, who continued to alternate seasons between the theaters. A 2002 windstorm ripped off some of the screen tower's plywood panels. The screen tower hung in there for a few more years, but by 2018, it was gone.

Sterling

In 1873, the first homesteaders in Sterling settled there. That is, they went to Union Colony, later called Greeley, but found the best land taken so they settled for Sterling. Railroad surveyor David Leavitt soon joined them and named their settlement after his home town of

Sterling IL. In 1880, another of those homesteaders offered Union Pacific Railroad 80 acres if it would build a depot and roundhouse there. That worked; Sterling incorporated in 1884 and became the seat of Logan County in 1887.

Starlite Drive-In

Opened: April 15, 1950

Closed: 2012

Capacity: 350 cars

Frank Childs, a longtime film salesman, decided to build his own drive-in a mile west of Sterling in 1949. He built the screen tower that fall, got the ticket office and projection booth set up, then quit his job and started the Starlite. In July 1952, a hail storm destroyed the Starlite's screen, but Childs rebuilt.

By 1997, the Starlite was down to one active screen, although both screens and their signs were still up. Photo by the author.

One of the ways scofflaws used to sneak into drive-ins was to enter through the exit, bypassing the ticket office. Starlite projectionist Orville W. Rupe invented a way to stop that, and you've probably encountered its descendant if you've ever rented a car. Rupe's patented device allowed anyone to drive over it in the expected direction, but anyone driving the opposite way would experience severe tire damage. The Starlite began using the device at the start of the 1953 season, freeing up the employee who had been tasked to keep watch at the exit. *Boxoffice* reported that several other drive-ins ordered their own copies of Rupe's work.

Before the 1960 season, Childs built a new, more colorful boxoffice at the Starlite. In 1966, he sold the drive-in to Paul Cory of Riverton WY. By 1974, Cory also ran the indoor Fox and Center in Sterling.

Orville Rupe stands behind his invention, the one-way exit gate with tire-ripping steel flanges, in this *Boxoffice* photo.

The Starlite kept running for the next few decades, but some of its details are fuzzy. Between 1985 and 1990, it added a second screen, though it had stopped showing movies on that second screen by 1997.

Somewhere along the way, Jack South bought it, and in 2008, he closed it. In early 2009, South told Troy Schott that he was selling the Fox and would throw in the Starlite. After Schott took him up on that offer, locals started a "Save the Starlite Fund," although Schott said he'd reopen it no matter how much the fund contributed. "Re-doing the drive-in theater will consist of an all new concession area and bathrooms in addition to other requirements by the health department," he told the *Sterling Journal-Advocate*.

After all that work, the Starlite didn't stay reopened very long. It closed after the 2012 season. Storage units occupy part of the old viewing field, but the screens and the entrance signs are still there.

Thornton

Compared to most of the cities in this book, Thornton is a youngster. It was effectively pure farmland in 1953 when Sam Hoffman laid out a planned community there, named after then-governor Dan Thornton. By 1960, it already held over 11,000 residents, and today its population is over 10 times that number.

North Star Drive-In

Opened: June 30, 1961

Closed: 1993

Capacity: 2000 cars

The North Star was Wolfberg Theatres' first drive-in of the 1960s, when the company expanded its drive-in roster to stay close to booming suburbs. The company broke ground on the project in November 1960 on 84th Avenue just west of the Valley Highway – then US 87, now I-25.

When it opened the following summer, the North Star was huge. Its 134x72-foot screen, said to be the largest in the Denver area, was covered in sheets of corrugated aluminum. Its lot, the largest west of Chicago, held 1600 cars on terraced ramps in an amphitheater style, keeping the viewing angle relatively level. Wolfberg district manager Leonard Albertini, who managed the East when it opened, designed the ramp system to take advantage of the site's natural slope.

The projection booth, on the second floor of the concession building, was over 550 feet away from the screen. Universal projectors inside could handle 70mm

The North Star sign's elevated star looks all the higher when compared to the ground-based Burger King sign behind it. Photo by Kenneth James Mitchell.

or 35mm film, though the company praised the brightness and higher definition of 70mm movies. The sound was also supposed to be better than average, delivered to specially designed Reed in-car speakers.

The North Star could handle a lot of people at once. Two box offices served four lanes of incoming traffic. At the concession stand, two piped guide rails directed patrons along cafeteria lines to a single cashier stand. Wolfberg kept the number of food choices deliberately low to keep the lines moving.

The 1962 *Theatre Catalog* included this photo of the huge 70/35 mm projector required for the 552-foot "throw" from the booth to the wide screen.

Customers could take that food to picnic tables in the 40,000-square foot Kiddie Korral directly behind the concession stand. The playground had the standard complement of whirls, swings, seesaws, and an elephant slide.

The North Star attracted plenty of customers for decades. When Commonwealth took over the Wolfberg chain in 1979, that included the North Star, which somehow saw its capacity grow to 2000 cars. In 1987, the drive-in city manager for Commonwealth told the *Denver Post* that the North Star still drew capacity crowds, even at that size, almost every weekend. Despite that success, its land became too valuable for the owners to resist selling. It closed after the 1993 season.

Trinidad

Established in 1861 along the Mountain branch of the Santa Fé Trail, Trinidad may have been named for one of early settler Felipe Baca's daughters. It soon flourished because of its location near Raton Pass and nearby coal mines. It experienced an economic decline in the early twentieth century, which saved many of its historic brick buildings from redevelopment. Trinidad's current economic boom again relied on its location as the southern gateway to Colorado, this time fueled by the state's legalization of marijuana in 2014.

Peak Drive-In

Opened: October? 1949

Closed: October? 1987

Capacity: 350 cars

In late 1949, 68-year-old Syrian immigrant Nathan Sawaya, a longtime Trinidad resident, built the town's only drive-in on state highway 350 near the municipal power plant. It opened in October that year for a brief run before closing for the season.

By 1951, the Peak was holding "Saturday Midnight Jam Session Jamborees," adding a band performance to the movie at no extra charge. I'll bet that had something to do with Nathan's oldest son George, a well-known jazz musician.

The Peak seemed almost perfectly preserved in 2003. Photo by Anthony L. Vazquez-Hernandez.

Nathan's wife passed away in 1951, and he died in 1957 after a long illness. By then, his youngest son, John Nathan Sawaya, was running the Peak and the indoor Strand.

In 2015, the Peak's box-office looked like it could a fresh coat of paint. Photo by Anthony L. Vazquez-Hernandez.

The Peak continued operating into the 1980s. Around 1986, a storm blew down its screen, but the younger Sawaya replaced it. Just after the 1987 season, he passed away at the age of 63. Even with its new screen, the Peak closed forever.

There should be an asterisk on that "forever." After a few decades of staying well-preserved in the dry climate, the Peak may get another life. Kenneth and Robert Beck founded Peak Cinemas to operate a local indoor theater, and their web site says that they hope that will become "our stepping stone to reviving the magic of the Drive-In theater, aiming to restore The Peak Drive-In to its glory days with a family oriented environment." I look forward to the reborn Peak.

Walsenburg

Walsenburg was originally settled in the early 1950s as La Plaza de los Leones, named for Don Miguel Antonio de Leon. But when the city formally incorporated in 1873, it took its name from Fred Walsen, a German immigrant who managed the local general store and later opened the county's first coal mine. The mines multiplied, and by the end of the 19th Century, Walsenburg was being called a "City Built on Coal."

Trail Drive-In

Opened: July 5, 1963

Closed: 1998?

Capacity: 300 cars

Frank Piazza, who had run indoor theaters in the county for decades, started building his drive-in five miles west of town in the winter of 1962-63. On Jan. 29, 1963, a strong wind totaled the screen, ripping it from its steel frame. Piazza rebuilt the screen, holding a soft opening in the first weekend of July before a "gala grand opening" on Wed., July 10.

The Trail held 300 cars with "plenty of room for expansion." Patrons facing the screen could see the Spanish Peaks in the background. The in-car speakers were built by Piazza's friend Sam Reed at the Reed Speaker Service in Golden.

The following summer, Piazza regraded the ramps at the Trail to fix a drainage problem. In July 1966, he held a special "New Year's Eve

Most of the Trail's sign was still there in 1997. By 2007, only the wooden platform was left. Photo by Kevin Dennis, all rights reserved. Used by permission.

in July" show complete with hats and party favors. And in March 1971, Piazza had to rebuild the screen again after yet another windstorm had destroyed the old one.

Eventually, Piazza retired, and the Trail went idle. A self-storage company occupies the site today, and it looks like it kept the old concession-projection building.

Westminster

In 1870, Pleasant DeSpain was the first settler in what became known as DeSpain Junction. Real estate developer C.J. Harris renamed the town Harris about 20 years later. That was about the time when Henry T. Mayham started the slow process of building Westminster University of Colorado, which opened in 1908. Three years later, when Harris voted to incorporate as a city, it took the name Westminster in honor of the university.

Motorena / North Drive-In

Opened: July 17, 1948

Closed: Sept. 21, 1996

Capacity: 800 cars

Less than a year after building the Denver area's first drive-in, the East, John Wolfberg started building two more – the West and one on Federal Blvd. north of town. But Wolfberg's Federal project died because somehow Irving Gilman's Carvue Theatres beat him to it, opening the Motorena at 72nd and Federal on the same day Wolfberg opened the West.

The Motorena "sacrificed parking area," Gilman said, to make room for a lighted central aisle to allow patrons to walk to one of the snack shops, located in front and back. An artesian well fed several drinking

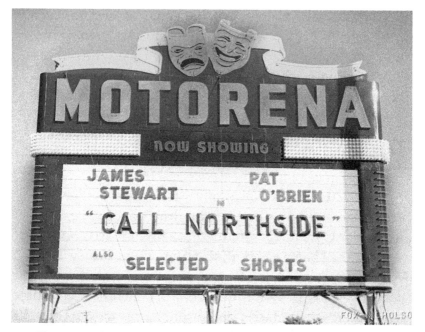

This 1948 photo of the original Motorena sign in Westminster was black and white, then marked with colors to suggest what it looked like when it was lit at night. Photo courtesy of the Gordon Sign Company.

fountains; customers were welcome to bring their own containers to carry water back home. The screen tower had seven-foot letters spelling out "Motorena" 65 feet up.

Wolfberg wasn't shut out for long, purchasing the Motorena in September 1948 and promptly renaming it the North. He also installed a playground. And then the company quietly ran the drive-in with only minor bits of news for the next 48 years. In May 1953, it was the first area drive-in to show a 3D movie, *Man in the Dark*. The North widened its screen before the 1955 season. A windstorm damaged that screen in March 1963, but after a few weeks, the North reopened.

From there, the North led a quiet, corporate-owned life. It was one of the last of the Wolfberg Compass drive-ins to close, at the end of the 1996 season.

The End (No X, Y, or Z)

That's all of the cities and towns of Colorado that ever had a drive-in theater. Thanks for reading all of their stories.

Would you like to read about more drive-ins?

You've read about every Colorado drive-in, but there's another book with 101 more history capsules:

Drive-Ins of Route 66

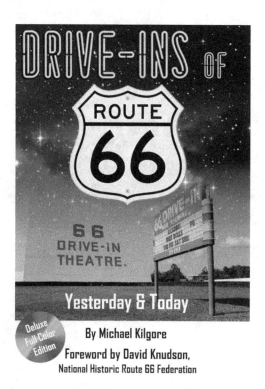

Available on Amazon Kindle and in full-color paperback. (Also in cheaper, ugly monochrome, but trust me, the color version is worth the difference.)

Bonus Gallery

Lucky you! In assembling the photos I could find (and legally use) for this book, I wound up with more than I could fit into the chapter with all the drive-in stories. So here are more glimpses into these great ozoners' pasts.

We'll start with the Island Acres site in Gunnison. In a 2012 photo by Pam Williams, above, the drive-in screen was still watching the old field. By 2019, only the screen's supports remained, as shown in the below photo by the author.

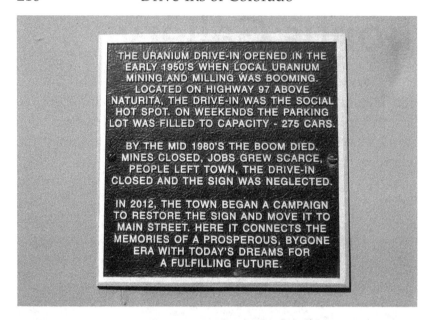

THE URANIUM DRIVE-IN OPENED IN THE
EARLY 1950'S WHEN LOCAL URANIUM
MINING AND MILLING WAS BOOMING.
LOCATED ON HIGHWAY 97 ABOVE
NATURITA, THE DRIVE-IN WAS THE SOCIAL
HOT SPOT. ON WEEKENDS THE PARKING
LOT WAS FILLED TO CAPACITY - 275 CARS.

BY THE MID 1980'S THE BOOM DIED.
MINES CLOSED, JOBS GREW SCARCE,
PEOPLE LEFT TOWN, THE DRIVE-IN
CLOSED AND THE SIGN WAS NEGLECTED.

IN 2012, THE TOWN BEGAN A CAMPAIGN
TO RESTORE THE SIGN AND MOVE IT TO
MAIN STREET. HERE IT CONNECTS THE
MEMORIES OF A PROSPEROUS, BYGONE
ERA WITH TODAY'S DREAMS FOR
A FULFILLING FUTURE.

Above, the plaque attached to the restored Uranium Drive-In sign, now in the middle of Naturita. Below, the view of Delta's Big Sky drive-in screen from the remains of its old projection building. 2019 photos by the author.

The 1954-55 *Theatre Catalog* included more photos of the
Wadsworth in Arvada than could fit in its entry. Above is an
exterior view of the auditorium that held over 500 theater
seats for customers who wanted an indoor movie experience
at the drive-in. Could that be why it was so financially
troubled? Below we see three box offices with the
auditorium in the background. On the left is just enough of
the screen to prove that its Lee Theatres ad (Page 26) might
have been misleading; the Wadsworth didn't have an arched
background when it opened.

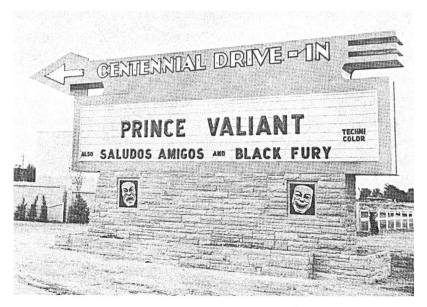

Here are two more from the 1954-55 *Theatre Catalog*, this time of the Centennial in Littleton. I'm partial to sign photos such as the one above, though I wonder how workers laid out the movie titles when both screens were active. Below is an early example of the twin cafeteria layout that soon became common. Check out the "Zero Burger" sign; their promotion of the Mr. Zero character extended even to the snack bar.

The wings of the North's screen expansion are obvious in the above photo. The off-center "NORTH" lettering suggests that Wolfberg left the middle two letters of "MOTORENA" in place when they renamed it. Below, a color view of the Lake Shore sign in front of its replacement metal screen. Both photos by Kenneth James Mitchell.

Even if I do say so, I love all of the elements of the Buena Vista Comanche photo above. The wildflowers at the base of the sign. The slightly worn paint job. The Sheep Mountain peaks in the distance. Below is the east face of the Fort Morgan Valley sign. Both photos by the author.

Three of the pioneers of Denver-area drive-ins were in this
1948 *Boxoffice* photo. Left to right, they were John Wolfberg,
his father Harris Wolfberg, and local manager Mickey Gross.
Real estate dealer B. B. Harding is the guy on the right.

Distant mountains and blue skies are my favorite backdrop,
whether for the Paonia (left, 2019) or Center's Frontier (right,
1999). Photos by the author.

Above: I love taking pictures of drive-in signs, but I don't take enough photos of box offices. Carol Highsmith's photo of the Mesa's in Pueblo helps correct that.
Below: Most photos of the Mesa's sign are of its east side, where the wide driveway provides a clear shot. It's harder to get a good photo from the west side, such as this one, because there's a strip mall and a wooden fence in the way. Both 2015 photos are from the Gates Frontiers Fund Colorado Collection within the Carol M. Highsmith Archive, Library of Congress, Prints and Photographs Division.

Acknowledgments

Writing this kind of book is like building a screen tower of bricks. So many people contributed so many pieces to the book, and my job has been to lay those bricks in place and keep the lines straight.

I want to thank everyone who helped, and I apologize in advance to anyone that I have left out of the following list. (If that's you, please remind me so I can include you in an updated version!)

Thanks to:

Kenneth James Mitchell for his photos and for being a sounding board. It was so nice to find someone else who speaks drive-in history.

The Colorado Historical Society, AKA History Colorado. Their friendly assistance in providing dozens of reels of microfilm allowed me to find stories in the state's old newspapers.

Mike Wolfe, who included a small sample of his unpublished Colorado drive-in book in a 2007 issue of *Colorado Heritage*. His lengthy descriptions of a few drive-ins inspired me to dig deeper and find more to write about.

Joe Bob Briggs, who has been a friend of Carload.com almost since its inception. It's always great when your heroes aren't jerks.

James Lane, for allowing me to use a photo of his iconic Tru Vu Drive-In on the cover.

Dr. Ellen McCormick, who came through at the last minute with great photos of Cañon City's Sunset.

Jeff Johnson, who supplied two great photos of Monte Vista's Star.

The Pikes Peak Library District, which has hundreds of great photos (not all of drive-ins) hosted online.

Lesley Struc at the Fort Collins Museum of Discovery, which also hosts online photos.

Matti Fisher of the Loyd Files Research Library in Grand Junction. She couldn't supply any photos but sent some superb oral histories of the state's second drive-in.

Jeana Johnson of the Fort Sedgwick Historical Society for her extensive, generous help with photos and information about Julesburg's Arrow.

Pam Williams, Larry McDonald, and David Primus for supplying photos and pointing me to more info about the Island Acres in Gunnison.

Andres S. "Pabblo" Carlos and Charles DiFerdinardo at the Animas Museum in Durango for their photos and memories of the Basin / Knox / Bell.

Todd Ellison, records administrator for the city of Durango, for assuring me that I could use the city's old Rocket photos, which it hosts online.

John Groy of the Comanche Drive-In in Buena Vista, for taking the time to pass along his knowledge of his drive-in and his folks' former drive-in in Salida. And for keeping the Comanche alive, of course.

(Now that I think of it, thanks to every drive-in theater owner and worker for helping to keep their theaters alive for another generation to experience.)

Lee Hallberg of the Mancos Public Library for helping me chase down an "almost" drive-in there.

Kurtis Klinghammer of Holly, for assuring me that "Pinky's" was a restaurant, and for pointing out the remains of the Kar-Vu east of Lamar.

Laura Whitt, Ignacio historian, for providing more details about the Buckskin's later days.

Steve Fitch, who allowed me to use his magnificent photo of the Star-Vu. I'd love to see more!

Chris Larson, library/museum supervisor for the city of Buckeye AZ, for providing a lot of leg work for just a short mention about Dove Creek's Auto Vu's founders.

Brianne Schreck and Sheryl Johnson from the Brighton City Museum for getting me the grand opening photo of the Kar-Vu.

Max Fulton of the Gordon Sign Company, for giving me free reign to search through and use his photos.

Arlene Shovald, Earle Kittleman, and Joy Jackson, for digging up great newspaper clippings and other memorabilia for the Groy and the Comanche.

Jeff Teasley and the rest of the HistoricAerials.com crew for letting me use their photos.

I am haunted by the near-certainty that I've left someone out. I so appreciate everyone who helped make sure that their town's drive-in stories were told here.

And of course, I need to thank my loving family for allowing and even encouraging so much effort on such a lightly regarded topic.

Graphics Notes

The front cover image was assembled by the author using the following ingredients:

Neon Green Light Alphabet Vector Font © Epifant-sev / Depositphotos.

Deep space © titoOnz / Depositphotos.

Colorado shield © BigAlBaloo / Depositphotos.

Author's 2017 photo of the Tru Vu Drive-In, Delta CO.

Special retro letter heading graphics are all © TeddyandMia / Depositphotos.

Some newspaper advertisements were color-corrected for greater legibility.

All of John Margolies's photos are from the John Margolies Roadside America photograph archive (1972-2008), Library of Congress, Prints and Photographs Division.

Licensed via Creative Commons (3.0):

The photo of the Aurora East (though it wasn't called that yet) by Greg Albertini.

The Springfield Kar-Vu photo by dallasmovie-theaters.

Licensed via Creative Commons (2.0):

The Boulder Holiday photo by Tadson Bussey. It was scaled and lightened for publication.

The Evans photo by Anthony L. Vazquez-Hernandez. It was scaled and spell-corrected for publication.

The chicken ranch photo (yes, this book actually has a chicken ranch photo) from the Orange County (CA) Archives.

The Valley photo by jeterga.

The Grand Junction Chief poster photo by "Nick" (Nick Genova).

The old TV photo by tomislav medak in A Short History of Drive-Ins.

Index

About the Author

Michael Kilgore is the webmaster of Carload.com, a drive-in theater information source since 1998. He has been recognized as a drive-in researcher by the Library of Congress. Previously, he was a writer and editor at the *Kansas City Star* and other newspapers. In 2019, he wrote *Drive-Ins of Route 66*, available on Amazon.com.